7-1-63

MINIATURE BULBS

by the same author

★

ANEMONES: FOR MARKET AND GARDEN
BULBS ALL THE YEAR ROUND
FRUIT ALL THE YEAR ROUND

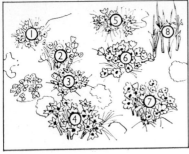

1. Crocus chrysanthus 'Warley White'
2. C. chrysanthus 'E. A. Bowles'
3. C. Sieberi 'Violet Queen'
4. C. susianus
5. C. chrysanthus 'Blue Pearl'
6. C. chrysanthus 'Peace'
7. C. chrysanthus 'Cream Beauty'
8. Iris reticulata 'Royal Blue'

MINIATURE BULBS

ROY GENDERS

ST MARTIN'S PRESS
New York

Printed in Great Britain
Library of Congress Catalog Card Number 63–11344

First published in the United States of America 1963

Introduction

For years I have been planting miniature bulbs in every available corner of my garden as well as in pots and pans for indoor colour throughout the year. For this reason, the writing of this book has been a labour of love, for I have tried to give a faithful description of all the true miniature bulbs, that is to say, those which grow less than twelve inches high, which I have come to know and love so well. In certain gardens there might be a slight variation in flowering times, but otherwise I think the descriptions will prove accurate. Yet, no matter what I write, the lovely photographs (taken by Mr. John Gledhill) of miniature bulbs growing in my home and garden convey the character and beauty of the plants so much more satisfactorily than mere words. And naturally their full charm may only be appreciated when they are actually seen in bloom. The miniatures are just right for the modern garden of limited size, and the blooms, whether cut and arranged in tiny jars or growing in small pots and pans, are ideal for decorating the small room.

My thanks are due to Mr. Lawrence Hills for guiding me throughout the writing of this book and for making most valuable suggestions; to Mr. John Gledhill for his patience with his photography; and to Doris Gatling for the preparation of the manuscript in her usual efficient style.

ROY GENDERS

Contents

7

CONTENTS

Part Two

Illustrations

9

ILLUSTRATIONS

10

ILLUSTRATIONS

Part One

Part One

CHAPTER 1

An Introduction to Miniature Bulbs

As ideal plants for the small garden—Introduction of the miniature bulbs—Characteristics—Hardiness—For indoor decoration—Buying miniature bulbs

Tall erect tulips, stiff and heavy hyacinths and large-flowered daffodils have for years provided striking spring displays in our great parks and country-house gardens; but in the modern garden of limited size, and in the window box or indoor pots of the small town flat, they are nothing like as suitable as the miniature bulbs, a selection of which will give colour the whole year round. The miniatures have a daintiness to be found in few other plants, and they may be expected to give pleasure for many years in return for a moderate original outlay.

As ideal plants for the small garden

Even taking into account their daintiness of habit where grown outdoors, miniatures will provide a brighter display, in proportion to the amount of ground they occupy, than any other plants. As an example, a dozen dwarf irises, or a dozen scillas, could be planted so as to occupy no more ground than a dinner plate would cover, and for weeks on end will illuminate that small space with brilliant colour; and when they have finished flowering, their foliage may be covered, as it dies back, with suitable miniature plants grown for their compact habit and freedom of flowering. For the small garden, then, the miniature bulbs are indispensable plants, and by planting the various species you will be able to provide a year-long display. Moreover, if your garden is to be as labour-saving as possible, they should be planted as liberally as your pocket permits.

AN INTRODUCTION TO MINIATURE BULBS

Introduction of the miniature bulb

It was almost five hundred years ago, when travellers began to leave this country in search of trade, that many of the species were first introduced to Britain. They came from Southern Europe, from the Iberian Peninsula and from the Middle East, and it may be said that the miniature flowering bulbs were more appreciated as a novelty than at any time since. By the beginning of the seventeenth century, however, very large sums were being paid for new introductions, and so great was the interest in them that in his *Paradisus*, published in 1629, Parkinson (then botanist to Charles I) devoted two hundred pages to complete descriptions and detailed illustrations of the many bulbous plants then to be found growing in Britain. They were ideal for the cottage gardens and for the dainty 'knot' gardens of the manor houses, but from then onwards most of the houses being built for the wealthy were large, their gardens were equally pretentious, and this trend continued during Georgian and Victorian times. The result was that the miniature flowering bulbs now had to make way for those with larger blooms and of taller habit.

That this ousting of the small flowering bulb was almost complete by the end of the eighteenth century is evident from M'Intosh's book, *The Flower Garden*. M'Intosh was gardener to the King of the Belgians when he published his famous work in 1838; and of more than five hundred pages, only two are devoted to a description of a few of the miniature flowering bulbs. Clearly, they had fallen into disfavour, but now, with the advent of the small modern house and its equally small garden, the miniature bulbs have once again come into their own. Likewise, other small flowering plants are becoming just as popular with the town gardener—they have long been cherished in the garden of the country cottager. We have seen the revival of the primrose in its many quaint forms, and of the pansy and viola, but many gardeners do not yet know of the miniature bulbs, apart from snowdrops and crocuses. Perhaps this is because such miniatures are rarely used by our Park Superintendents, and at the Shows they are somewhat inconspicuous when displayed alongside plants which have so much larger blooms and thus make a more brilliant display. When newly introduced, these miniature bulbs must have been quite costly, but it is not just the question of expense which prevents their wider planting nowadays.

16

1. *Galanthus Ikariae.* An outstanding species having very large flowers—the inner petals marked with bright green crescents—and possessing a rich perfume. Flowers February–March

2. *Galanthus*, 'Arnott's Seedling'

3. *Galanthus nivalis*. The Snowdrop

4. A drift of Golden Garlic (*Allium moly*)

AN INTRODUCTION TO MINIATURE BULBS

Characteristics

Those who are interested in these dainty flowering bulbs will be well rewarded by a visit to Kew; to the Botanical Gardens in Edinburgh; or to the gardens of the Northern Horticultural Society at Harrogate where, almost throughout the year, in the alpine gardens and beneath trees where grass refuses to grow, also on low banks where the grass is kept short, and in those odd sunless corners to be found in most gardens, the miniature bulbs will be seen flowering in all their glory. Once seen growing some distance away from their more robust relations, they will take on a greater beauty, their dainty and informal habit giving them a charm all their own.

That they are far longer lasting than the large flowering bulbs is an important consideration. The tulips, for instance, which are used for late spring and early summer bedding, quickly deteriorate, the blooms becoming smaller and smaller with each year; and so it is necessary to renew them, if not every year, certainly in alternate years if the display is to be maintained. With the little tulip species, which are so attractive where planted about a rockery or in short grass, the bulbs multiply like those of the daffodil and seem to gather strength as the years pass by, increasing the display with little or no attention. Thus there is not only a considerable saving of labour but also of expense. Indeed, most of the miniature bulbs multiply with great rapidity and a mere dozen bulbs will have increased four-fold within two or three years, if soil and situation are acceptable to them. Nor will they require lifting and dividing until the clumps, over-crowded, are becoming less prolific in their flowering.

Phillip Miller, who was appointed Curator of the Chelsea Physic Garden in 1722, advised against lifting miniature bulbs more than absolutely necessary, for their flowering would be sparse until they had re-established themselves. The miniatures may justly be considered to be as permanent as are trees and shrubs, and to demand as little attention.

Hardiness

Other valuable qualities of most of the miniature bulbs are their extreme hardiness and their ability to bloom in shade. Those whose garden is exposed to strong winds, or is low-lying and exposed to late frosts, will find the dwarf bulbs well able to tolerate such adverse conditions. In an exposed garden everything should be done to provide the plants with as much shelter as possible, by planting them around the base of mature trees or close to the stones of a rockery. Where this is not possible the blooms will come to little harm, for most of them grow less than eight inches tall, and in spite of the somewhat frail appearance of some of them, will prove well able to withstand the strongest winds. I have known beds of May-flowering tulips to be decapitated in a severe gale while dwarf bulbs growing nearby remained unscathed.

Neither will hard frost cause them much harm, and none at all where the bulbs can be given the protection of low-growing shrubs, or of the overhanging branches of trees, or of rockery stone. What is more, the miniature bulbs will grow where few other plants could be brought into bloom, in the shade of mature trees, or in the shade cast by nearby houses or buildings. This, to a town gardener, is of the utmost importance, for shade is so often the greatest difficulty that he has to encounter. Almost all the bulbs mentioned in this book, with one or two exceptions such as the Poppy Anemones, the irises, and several of the tulip species, in addition to those half-hardy bulbs of South African origin, will flourish in shade; and this will greatly prolong the flowering period. Bulbs may be planted in those parts of the garden unsuitable for other plants which may be grown in the more favourable sites, leaving the miniature bulbs to brighten the dullest corners.

But charming as are the miniature bulbs when planted about the garden and on the rockery, they will give even more pleasure where they are growing close to the eye, for only then may the fullness of their beauty be fully appreciated. In the trough garden raised above ground level, in the window box, and where growing in small pots and bowls in the alpine house and indoors, the blooms may be observed in detail. The beauty of the delightful little Lebanon Squill, *Puschkinia scilloides*, may be enjoyed to the full only where observed at close quarters, for the bluish-white blooms, no larger than the size of a sixpenny piece, are most attractively striped with soft, clear blue down the centre and sides of each petal to give the blooms a heavenly blue appearance. The beauty of *Crocus laevigatus* depends on similar delicate features, its rosy-mauve flowers being shaded with buff and feathered with purple on the exterior, so that each bloom has the appearance of having been painted by hand. So, wherever possible, grow them indoors as well as in the garden, for indoors they will be seen in bloom several weeks before they will flower outdoors, thus giving several additional weeks of beauty.

For indoor decoration

The miniature bulbs are ideal for the small modern room, for a dozen bulbs may be planted in only a small bowl to provide a display of great charm; and where they have been grown well, and have not become 'drawn', they should not require supporting in the same way as will most of the taller-growing bulbs. A number of the miniatures possess a powerful fragrance, so that no more than half a dozen blooms will scent a room. Tiny indoor gardens may be constructed in pans using the miniature bulbs and small pieces of rock-like stone. The bulbs should be planted in groups of three or four to give a succession of bloom throughout winter and spring. And all they require is a dark cupboard in which to root and a window in which to bloom, and an occasional watering to maintain the compost in a moist condition.

Many of the miniature bulbs also furnish cut flowers. Small earthenware jars should be used for display, since the blooms will have only short stems and tiny heads and the containers must be in proportion. Jars of mixed flowers are most attractive; try mixing the tiny blue scillas with the miniature golden daffodils. Snowdrops and chionodoxas blend equally well together, and they may be enhanced by a few small sprays of the golden winter jasmine or forsythia. Though so tiny, the blooms will drink copiously, so remember to fill up the jars each day. And if the bloom can be kept in a cool room it will last considerably longer than in heat.

As I write this chapter, the lovely *Iris Danfordiae*, with its blooms of brilliant gold borne on only three-inch stems, is just unfolding its flowers during the first warm February sunshine. In the orchard, the snowdrops are already in full bloom, and on the low bank through which a path has been cut to the house, the delightful *Crocus ancyrensis* is just appearing, its bright orange cups stippled with bronze on the outside. Growing near them, the tiny daffodil *Narcissus minimus* is showing colour, its fairy-like trumpet of rich yellow held on a stem only about two inches high.

Even in a large garden these little gems, if planted in large groups, command immediate attention. One looks for them daily, almost hourly, as they are expected to come into bloom, and this pleasant

19

pastime continues the whole year round. Even on the darkest days of November, when the ground is wet and cold and the mist has spread its chilly blanket over the garden, many lovely miniature bulbs will be in bloom. Beneath the mature trees, nestling about the exposed roots, a few of the rosy-pink butterfly-like flowers of *Cyclamen neapolitanum* may still be seen, and near to them are to be found drifts of the winter-flowering crocus species, the fragrant *Crocus longiflorus* with its flowers of soft lilac, and *Crocus ochroleucus* with its cream-coloured blooms of striking orange base. In the shrubbery the colchicums continue to bloom, the first having made their appearance at the end of August. Rarely will there be a week in the year when at least one of the charming miniature bulbs will not be showing flowers. The Northamptonshire poet John Clare, in his 'Approach of Spring', tells of the thrill of finding new flowers:

> . . . *What lovely prospects wait each waking hour,*
> *When each new day some novelty displays:*
> *How sweet the sunbeam melts the crocus flower,*
> *Whose borrow'd pride shines dizen'd in his rays.*

With the miniature bulbs, every season has 'lovely prospects', for they are to be enjoyed throughout the year, and never are these intimate little plants more appreciated than in times of sorrow or distress, greeting the beholder with their simple beauty and bringing with them new hope. And one of their most rewarding features is that they will not only return next year in unimpaired glory, as richly coloured as ever, but will return in even greater abundance.

Buying miniature bulbs

As many of the species as possible should be obtained, for in this way one may enjoy bloom throughout the year; and as almost all are of some particular habit, they also differ greatly as to colour and form. Flowering at heights extending from two to twelve inches, they are suitable for a variety of habitats, but care must be taken to obtain them from a reliable supplier. Many of them are so small that there will be little latitude for decay or damage from poor storage; the margin is naturally wider in the case of large bulbs which in some cases will be ten times (or more) greater in size. Small bulbs which have been lifted carelessly and thereby bruised or cut, and those which have shrivelled as a result of being stored in too dry an atmosphere, must be avoided, for they will never make vigorous growth. The bulbs should have been dried and stored with care and at planting time should be quite firm when pressed between finger and thumb. They must have a plump appearance which will not be the case if they were lifted too soon after flowering. The big chaps may put up quite a brave show if not of first-rate quality, but poor condition will be fatal to the miniatures. To sum up, they must be clean, fresh, plump and firm, and then they may be expected to give a vigorous display.

There is plenty of fun to be obtained from adding to one's collection of miniature bulbs each year, for the species and varieties are so numerous that it would be almost impossible to have them all. One or two species could be added to the collection each year, for there will be few places about the garden where space cannot be found for at least one or two. Certainly plant the large-flowering bulbs, but believe me when I say that the continued neglect of the miniatures is quite unbelievable when one considers their many valuable qualities, well recognized in Tudor and early Stuart times.

CHAPTER 2

Small Bulbs for Naturalising

A labour-saving garden—Planting in rough grass—Suitable bulbs for naturalising—Planting under trees

One of the most attractive gardens it has been my pleasure to enjoy during recent years had been made around a semi-detached suburban house occupying a corner position. First, over-lapping fencing six feet high was erected to give privacy. The outlay was quite considerable but this fence has saved many hours of laborious hedge clipping and given immediate privacy with no waiting for a hedge to make several years' growth. Around the inside of the fencing standard ornamental trees were planted, beneath which was sown an inexpensive grass mixture, though first the ground had been cleared of weeds and lavishly planted with bulbs. The trees and rough grass formed a belt almost ten feet wide, and after five years the trees had almost closed in to hide the fencing and to give a greater measure of seclusion.

A labour-saving garden

The coloured foliage of the maples in autumn, the blossom of the flowering cherries in spring, and the fruits of the crab apples and other berried trees during winter provided colour and interest almost throughout the year. Under the trees the bulbs added their full share of beauty. The rough grass was cut only in autumn, bulbs which bloom at this time of the year being confined to other parts of the garden. Inside the belt of trees a lawn was made and this also was planted with miniature bulbs to bloom from Christmas until Easter. The lawn could thus be cut and kept tidy from early June, when the foliage of the bulbs had died down, until the final cutting of the grass late in October. The autumn- and early winter-flowering bulbs were confined to a long narrow border and to the circles of soil cut out around the base of fruit trees. They were also planted in the ground

22

made bare by the branches of overhanging trees; here they are left quite undisturbed to die down after flowering. This was a labour-saving garden of great charm and my own garden, which covers several acres, has been laid out in similar fashion, marrying the formal with the informal; and during springtime especially, the bulbs produce a riot of colour without needing much attention.

There are three ways of growing small flowering bulbs in grass. They may be:

(a) planted in grass which is rough, is allowed to grow tall, and is cut only twice a year;

(b) planted in a lawn which must be kept neat and tidy;

or (c) planted in grass beneath tall trees, where lack of sunshine means that sparser grass will require little or no attention.

In each case choose vigorous, long-living bulbs and plant them where they will give the best display.

Planting in rough grass

Grass must be kept under control if the garden is to look tidy and the bulbs must be allowed time to die back naturally before any foliage is removed.

Bulbs in coarse grass should have finished flowering by the end of May. This will allow time for the foliage of the May-flowering blue-bell, the summer snowflake and the later-flowering tulip species to die down before the grass is cut and made tidy in summer. Autumn-flowering bulbs may also be planted in coarse grass, but choose those which bloom as early in autumn as possible. This will allow the foliage to die down before the grass is made tidy towards the year's end. Alternatively, the autumn-flowering bulbs may be confined to a corner of the coppice or orchard where the grass is cut in mid-summer only. For the same reason, bulbs for planting in a lawn should be those which finish flowering by the end of April so that their foliage has time to die back before it is necessary to give the grass its first cut.

If bulbs growing in grass are to remain vigorous and free flowering, as well as increasing each year, they must be treated with the utmost respect after flowering. This is the time when the sap from the leaves is returning to the bulb, and to allow it to do so gradually will mean a vigorous bulb, capable of continuing its reproduction and flowering the following year. If the foliage is removed too soon, the bulb will

23

quickly lose vitality and may stop flowering altogether. After flower-ing, most bulbous plants tend to become untidy, the leaves turning first yellow then brown, so that there is always the temptation to remove them before they have fully died back. For this reason, bulbs are best grown in a border or shrubbery, under mature trees where little else will grow, or around the base of small trees, where there will be no urgency about removing their foliage.

One should, of course, plant with a view to enjoying as long a period of flowering as possible but many of the miniature bulbs, those needing an open, sunny situation and those which bloom on too short a stem, will be quite unsuited for planting in coarse grass. Choose rather kinds which come into bloom late in spring, with others to continue the display through the summer and into autumn. Those blooming during mid-summer must be omitted where it is necessary to cut the grass after the late spring and early summer bulbs have died back. The orchard or wild garden could be at their most colourful with bulbs during April and May and again during Sep-tember and October, with the grass-cutting being done round about July 1st, at its point of maximum growth. At this date the late spring-flowering bulbs will have died back and those which are to bloom in autumn will not have begun to form their leaves. If cutting is delayed for more than a day or two, the autumn-flowering bulbs will be seriously damaged. The flowering season may be prolonged where it is also possible to plant miniature bulbs in short grass, for these little chaps flower during the first days of the New Year and provide colour until those growing in rough grass come into bloom.

Suitable bulbs for naturalising

First to bloom, the snowdrops must never be omitted from the wild garden, for there is nothing more pleasing than to find the first white blooms behind a tuft of grass on the first warm day of the year. Though most of the species are dwarf, the snowdrop is quite happy in long grass.

> *Sweet type of innocence, snow-clothèd blossom,*
> *Seemly, though vainly, bowing down to shun*
> *The storm hard-beating on thy wan white bosom . . .*
> *Ah, thou art winter's snowdrop, lovely Woman.*

So wrote John Clare in his lovely sonnet 'The Snowdrop'.

A 3-cm. bulb will produce a bloom during its first season but the best method of planting is to lift and divide the clumps immediately after flowering, replanting into grass with an ordinary trowel. Attractive as are the dwarf varieties for naturalising, those of taller habit should also be planted, though considerably more expensive. A form of *Galanthus nivalis*, Arnott's Seedling, bears it sweetly-perfumed flowers on 12-inch stems; *G. Allenii*, with its egg-shaped blooms, is also long in the stem. *G. imperati* '*Atkinsi*', which bears a long-petalled bloom on a 9-inch stem, is also valuable for the wild garden.

Similar are the snowflakes and both the spring- and summer-flowering snowflakes should be grown in the wild garden. *Leucojum vernum* grows little more than 7–8 inches tall, its pretty drooping bell-shaped flowers appearing before the end of March. It remains in bloom until early May when *L. aestivum*, Parkinson's 'Bulbous Violet' takes over, its elegant white flowers tipped with green appearing on 12-inch stems, often slightly taller.

Nor should the exquisite *Erythronium tuolumnense* be omitted, for it comes into bloom in March, before any other plant excepting the snowdrop; its yellow blooms, like golden butterflies, are borne on 12-inch stems: indeed a plant for the connoisseur, though of easy culture.

The Wood Lilies (Trilliums), natives of North America, are also delightful plants for a wild garden, loving shady places and a moist soil. They bloom during April and May (about 12 inches). One of the most interesting is *T. erectum*, with glossy, claret-coloured flowers of most disagreeable smell. Plant with it the 'Wake Robin', *T. grandiflorum*, which bears a large three-petalled bloom of purest white above handsome shiny leaves. Many of the bulbs so valuable for naturalising have white flowers, and their purity is accentuated by the green of the grass.

Yet another wild-garden bulb is the Star of Bethlehem, *Ornithogalum*, of which *O. narbonense* and *O. nutans*, flowering in early summer, are outstanding, bearing their spikes of silvery white on nine-inch stems, the blooms closing up with the approach of evening. They will flourish almost anywhere and like the *Sternbergia*, with which they grow in the Middle East, can thrive in a poor, dry soil.

A number of the taller-growing and more robust daffodils are admirable subjects for planting in coarse grass; those of smaller habit are best grown on a rockery, towards the front of a shrubbery, or amidst the short grass of a sunny bank. The Lent Lily, the Old English wild daffodil, which has a creamy white perianth and pale yellow trumpet, should be planted in profusion, for the bulbs are inexpensive. The blooms, on eight- to nine-inch stems, are delightful for cutting for small jars. Another, blooming early, is the lovely hybrid W. P. Milner, its almost pure white flowers borne on ten- to twelve-inch stems. Quite charming is the old *N. cernuus*, with blue-green foliage and nodding flowers of silvery white on ten-inch stems. The elegant *N. cyclamineus* hybrid, 'February Gold', with bright orange trumpets on twelve-inch stems during March, should also be planted; to continue the display until early June, plant *N. gracilis*, like a tiny Jonquil with sweetly-scented flowers. All the miniature daffodils take a year or more to become fully established, and they should be disturbed as little as possible.

In my garden the daintiest of the miniature daffodils are confined to two grassy banks almost six feet high between which a path has been cut. Here *N. minor* makes its appearance towards the end of March and the taller-flowering *N. gracilis* finishes blooming early in June, the last of the season. I advise planting in groups of six bulbs, not too deep, with the smallest at the top of the bank, the tallest at the bottom. With the daffodils in long grass, plant *Muscari latifolium*, a most distinctive Grape Hyacinth, bearing sky-blue and dark-blue bells on twelve-inch stems; it has attractive broad leaves, too.

The tulip species should always find a place in the wild garden, for they live longer as miniatures than as large-flowered Dutch hybrids used in vast numbers for bedding. They will multiply in the same way as the snowdrops, scillas and other naturalised bulbs. *T. praestans* is an excellent choice, and throughout April bears its brilliant orange-scarlet blooms three or four to a twelve-inch stem. To extend the season well into May choose *T. saxatilis*, with shining dark green leaves and flowers of a lovely shade of lilac, on ten-inch stems. Another handsome tulip is *T. Whittallii major*, which bridges the gap between the appearance of these two species. Its urn-shaped flowers are of vivid orange. Also suitable for planting in coarse grass is *T. orphanidea* from Greece. The pointed petals are of mahogany colour shaded with purple. I first saw the miniature tulip, planted in this way, with daffodils, down the avenue leading to the back of Trinity College, Cambridge, where their richly coloured blooms were a most effective foil for the more delicately coloured daffodils grown in their thousands along the 'Backs'. Like the daffodils, they are easy to grow and have a long flowering season.

Also for planting in coarse grass is the May-flowering *Allium kara-*

taviense, a most beautiful and interesting member of the garlic family, and although *A. moly* is always at its best in the shrubbery, it need not be excluded from the wild garden. Its metallic leaves are tinted with red and its ball-shaped flowers, on twelve-inch stems, are of a lovely shade of lilac-grey. Equally useful, and in bloom early in June, is the sweetly-scented White Garlic of Southern Europe, *A. neapolitanum*. Like *A. karataviense* it grows to twelve inches tall and is excellent for cutting, but as it flowers rather late it might be better in the shrubbery.

Choicest of all plants for the wild garden are the fritillaries, especially the Snake's-head Fritillary, its long, drooping flowers exquisitely mottled to resemble the head of a snake. *F. meleagris* in its numerous lovely forms flowers during May and has strong wiry stems. The blooms are far less fragile than they appear to be. *F. pallidiflora*, from Siberia, has yellow flowers beautifully chequered inside with purple. In olden times, *F. meleagris* was known as the Ginny Hen Flower, because its markings resembled those on the feathers of the Guineahen. It was later named *F. Caperonius*, after Noel Caperon, a Frenchman who found it growing in the meadows near Orleans. Parkinson sadly tells us that 'he was, shortly after the finding, taken away in the Massacre'.

There is quite a good choice of scillas, in blue, pink and white. The tiny *S. bifolia* and the Siberian Squill are best in border or rockery; the Spanish and English Wood Hyacinths, the familiar blue-bells of our woodlands, are best confined to the wild garden. Here they multiply with great rapidity, so much so that they will become a nuisance if planted in the border. *S. hispanica* is a more refined form of our native blue-bell. *S. nutans* 'Blue Queen' bears dozens of pyramidal spikes of porcelain-blue bells on twelve-inch stems. Plant with it but not too close, the beautiful white form, *alba*, and the delicate pink, 'Franz Hals', which grows slightly taller.

During the Middle Ages, scillas were known as 'Sea Onions', for the bulbous roots were taken to sea by sailors to be used as food. Often the plants were lifted with their foliage, and were strung up on board ship in the same way as onions. A writer of Stuart times said that the scilla 'is wholly used physically, because we can perseive no pleasure from the sight of the flower'!

For September and October flowering choose the beautiful Zephyr Flower, *Zephyranthes*; it has crocus-like flowers in profusion on ten-inch stems. It is quite hardy and likes some sun, but as it is native of the swamp-lands of Peru it must be planted in soil containing plenty of peat or leaf mould. *Z. candida*, which is not expensive, has lovely waxy white blooms amidst a forest of rush-like leaves. The new yellow flowering hybrid, 'Ajax', makes a useful companion for *Z. candida*. And the Autumn Snowflake, *Leucojum autumnale*, could well be planted with the *Zephyranthes*. It, too, has rush-like foliage, its drooping Snowdrop-like blooms are tinged with pink and borne on twelve-inch stems.

Planting under trees

In gardens with mature trees there will be the opportunity of planting the hardy cyclamen where they are always happiest, in those pockets formed around the boles of trees. They seem to enjoy the protection from cold winds afforded by the trees and will flourish in a light, loamy soil enriched with leaf mould. But they do like some lime rubble about their roots and some should be incorporated before the corms are planted just beneath the surface of the soil.

Where there is room, plant two or three corms each of half a dozen species and there will be flowers the whole year round apart from the four or five weeks of mid-summer. But it is during mid-winter, when the grass is short, that they will be most appreciated.

The hardy cyclamen is one of the few plants to grow well under conifers. Several of the species have blooms which are deliciously fragrant; when established, they seed themselves freely, forming close mats of crimson, pink and white; the leaves, with their silver markings, are also most striking.

The corms must not be too deeply planted; put no more than an inch of compost over them and make sure that you do not plant them upside down. The only exception is *C. europaeum*, which likes to be set deeper. Set the corms nine to ten inches apart so that established clumps will not be overcrowded. Plant the spring- and summer-flowering species in September and those that bloom in autumn and winter in July.

First to bloom, very early in spring, is *C. coum*, with rounded leaves of bottle green and small flowers of vivid carmine-red. There is also a lovely white form, *album*, which is scarce and hard to find. Then in April and May comes *C. repandum*, an exquisite plant with leaves marbled with silver and bright crimson flowers. For July and August, choose *C. europaeum*, with its sweetly-scented flowers of rosy-red, appearing before the leaves, and to follow *C. cilicium* with flowers of purest pink. *C. neapolitanum*, also for July and August, is worth planting for its foliage alone; it seems well able to survive with the minimum of moisture. For winter flowering there is *C. Atkinsii*, which produces its welcome pale carmine-pink flowers in a sheltered corner throughout the winter.

The Hardy cyclamen are also particularly attractive in the dell or woodland garden where the ground is almost fully shaded when the trees come into leaf. Here, the Dog's Tooth Violets and the Winter Aconite will flourish. The Woodland Anemone, *A. nemorosa*, will multiply rapidly, quickly covering the ground with its single white blooms. Plant with it, as generously as possible, the variety 'Royal Blue', which bears large flowers of a lovely shade of lavender-blue on six-inch stems. They will succeed the scillas and will be in bloom at the same time as the Wood Lily, *Trillium erectum*, with deep crimson flowers on twelve-inch stems. The flowers are large, the foliage luxuriant. One bulb will cost about the price of a packet of cigarettes, but will give years of pleasure. One or two carpeted with the white Wood Anemone will make a most arresting picture in the half shade of the dell.

The miniature daffodils and snowdrops will be perfectly happy in the woodland garden; so will *Tulipa sylvestris*, where the ground is not entirely shaded. Bulbs of *Corydalis cava* and *C. angustifolia*, with their graceful fern-like foliage, are also at home there, as are Solomon's Seal and various ferns. The foliage of the bulbs will die back almost unnoticed, hidden by the ferns and the foliage of the cyclamen and the *Erythronium*.

The less costly dwarf flowering bulbs, such as the Winter Aconites, Chionodoxas and Siberian Squills may be planted lavishly in rough grass to provide a carpet of colour as background for the taller subjects, but generally it is more satisfactory to confine them to pockets around trees and to short grass. They may also be planted in groups along the side of a small garden path, where they are visible in all weathers. Groups of the dainty *Scilla bifolia* (the shell-pink and the dark blue forms growing together), the sturdy little Grape Hyacinths (the purple *Muscari azureum* and the white form, *album*), *Iris reticulata* and some of the many crocuses will provide interest and colour for many weeks. To give an example: in my own garden there is a narrow winding path, nearly a hundred yards long, running from the entrance gate up to the house. Along one side crocuses have been planted in the short grass, as many as fifty different varieties being used. These have been planted in groups of separate varieties, each of a hundred bulbs (corms), and though they were not planted in rows, they form a band about two feet wide where the grass is not cut until several weeks after they have finished flowering. Those which bloom during autumn are planted together, likewise those which bloom during the winter and spring months, so that there is continuous colour excepting in the three mid-summer months; and they make a picture of quite outstanding beauty.

BULBS FOR PLANTING IN LONG GRASS

Name	Flowering Time	Height
Allium karataviense	May	10–12 ins.
Anthericum liliastrum	June–July	12 ins.
Brodiaea grandiflora	June	8 ins.
Erythronium californicum	April	12 ins.
„ tuolumnense	March	12 ins.
Fritillaria meleagris	April–May	12 ins.
Galanthus Arnott's Seedling	March	10 ins.
„ Elwesii	March	8–9 ins.
„ plicatus	March	8 ins.
Leucojum aestivum	May–June	12 ins.
„ vernum	March–May	6 ins.
Muscari comosum	April–May	12 ins.
„ latifolium	April–May	10 ins.
Narcissus cyclamineus	March	9 ins.
„ gracilis	May–June	12 ins.
„ lobularis	Feb–March	8–9 ins.
Ornithogalum nutans	May–June	8–9 ins.
„ umbellatum	May–June	6 ins.
Scilla amethystina	May–June	8–9 ins.
Trillium cernuum	April–May	12 ins.
„ grandiflorum	May–June	12 ins.
Tulipa chrysantha	May	8 ins.
„ Eichleri	April	10 ins.
„ Kolpakowskiana	April	9 ins.
„ primulina	April	9 ins.
„ saxatilis	May	9 ins.
Zephyranthes atamasco	May–June	7 ins.
„ candida	Aug–Sept	8 ins.

CHAPTER 3

Bulbs in the Lawn

The use of early flowering bulbs—Planting in grass—Correct planting depths—The Emerald Velvet lawn—A chamomile lawn—Bulbs for the waterside

F ortunately those bulbs which bloom early in spring are the smallest and daintiest of all and lend themselves admirably to planting in a lawn. As it will be necessary to cut the grass by early May at the latest, any bulbs in lawn grass should have finished flowering by early April; but where mature trees overhang a part of the lawn, thus checking the grass, later-flowering bulbs may also be grown. Summer- and autumn-flowering bulbs are not suitable for a lawn, for cutting would deprive them of their foliage.

The use of early-flowering bulbs

Bulbs planted in a lawn or beneath trees should be set out in generous drifts. Sun-lovers are naturally best in unshaded grass, the shade-tolerant ones under trees. The following will be quite happy in partial shade, for it must be remembered that when most of them are in bloom, the trees will not yet be fully clothed in their summer green:

Anemone nemorosa	*Hyacinthus amethystinus*
Corydalis cava	*Muscari botryoides*
Cyclamen neapolitanum	*Narcissus* species
Eranthis species	*Ornithogalum nutans*
Erythronium species	*Scilla* species
Galanthus species	

Though the bulbs will have finished flowering by mid-April, the foliage will not have died back by the time the grass is ready for its first cutting. But if tidiness matters, there is no harm done if you remove that portion of the foliage which has turned brown and will

31

by then have nothing to contribute to the future vigour of the bulb. Alternatively, the foliage may be kept reasonably tidy by tying it together into a loose knot. Until all the foliage has died down, it should never be removed close to the ground. This will mean that if a lawn is making more growth than usual during the early weeks of summer, you must compromise by cutting the grass around and between the bulbs wherever possible. For this reason it is better to plant in groups or drifts rather than here and there all over the lawn. Later, the blade of the mower may be raised as high as possible for the first cutting made over the bulbs when the foliage has almost died back. Afterwards, the lawn may be cut as closely as required, for by then the foliage will have played its part. If the foliage has to be removed before it has completely died back, removal should be gradual. Bulbs having large, coarse foliage should never be planted in a lawn but should be confined to the shrubbery.

Planting in grass

The bulbs should be planted after the grass has been cut reasonably short as late in autumn as possible. Planting will be easier and the grass will still be short when most of the spring bulbs are in bloom. Cutting late will also ensure that the grass will not require cutting again until early the following summer, when the foliage of the bulbs has had ample time to die back.

As selective weed killers of the hormone type, and based on MCPA potassium salt, are now widely used to keep a lawn free from weeds, their possible ill effects on bulbs must not be overlooked.

The weed killer Verdone may be safely used during autumn, when spring-flowering bulbs are dormant and the foliage has died back and has been removed. The preparation should not, however, be used when the leaves of the bulbs are showing above ground. In any case, autumn is the most effective time for using the selective weed killers, when the ground is still warm from the summer sunshine and the autumnal rains cause the weeds to make vigorous growth. One treatment given at this time of the year should be sufficient to keep the lawn free from weeds, and the bulbs will in no way be harmed.

There are two methods of planting. Either a section of turf is lifted by cutting it out with a sharp spade to the required measurements, or the bulbs are inserted singly, with a special bulb trowel or the bulb-planting tool marketed by Messrs. Wallace and Barr, suitable for

5. *Fritillaria meleagris*. The 'Chequered Daffodil' or 'Snakeshead Lily'

6. When possible bulbs should be planted on a layer of sharp sand. Here the *Scilla sibirica* is planted

7. Bulbs of the Winter Aconite (*Eranthis hyemalis*) are planted two inches deep and two inches apart on a layer of coarse sand

8. Tubers and Corms

Ranunculus　　　　　　　　　*Erythronium dens-canis*
Fritillaria meleagris　　　　　　　　*Tulipa biflora*

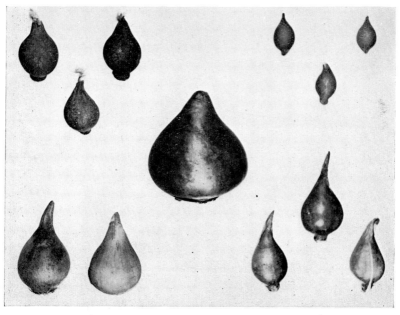

9. Bulbs of Miniature Tulips compared with bulbs of Dutch Tulip
Tulipa clusiana　　　　'Keizerskroon'　　　　*T. chrysantha*
　　T. tarda　　　　　　　　　　　　*T. sylvestris*

10. Tubers of *Oxalis adenophylla*

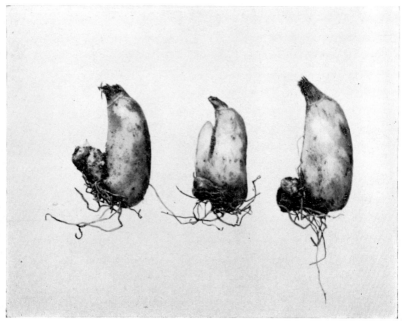

11. *Erythronium dens-canis*. 'Dog's Tooth Violet'

planting small bulbs and costing 65*s*. It will save much time and energy-expendituré where the garden is large. The bulb trowel costs only 10*s*. 6*d*. and is so designed that a small circular piece of turf, and soil to the correct depth, may be removed with ease. The bulb is then dropped in and the turf replaced and trodden firm.

Where a section of turf is removed with a spade, the soil should be stirred and a little peat and sand placed over the surface into which the bulbs will be pressed. Six to eight bulbs may be planted where about one square foot of turf has been removed, for we shall be dealing only with small bulbs, some very small indeed. Do not plant in straight lines, and do not remove the turves with geometrical exactitude, for you aim at a natural-looking arrangement: but bear in mind the warning already given about 'grouping' rather than 'dotting'. Where planting singly, set groups of half a dozen, spacing the bulbs several inches apart; and do not plant too closely, for overcrowding will soon occur.

As each opening is made in the ground, drop in a pinch of prepared compost before the bulb is placed into position (the right way up). It is important to ensure that the base of the bulb is actually in contact with the compost, so that the root action may begin promptly. If the bulb is in an air pocket it may not form satisfactory roots and will take longer to become established. For this reason a pointed tool should never be used for taking out a hole for bulbs. It is a good plan to mark out the ground by means of plant labels printed with the name of the bulb before any planting is done, so that the same ground will not be planted over more than once. Plan as you would before planting the herbaceous border, so that the purple-blue Grape Hyacinths may bloom with the yellow- and white-flowered miniature daffodils, and let the summer snowflakes mingle with the scillas in a separate part of the garden.

Bulbs are the ideal plants for the labour-saving garden, for even if for some reason the garden is left derelict for any length of time it will come alive again through its bulbs just as soon as a clearance has been made, even though almost all other plant life will have been choked out of existence.

Correct planting depths

Planting depths must not be haphazard, for though certain liberties may be taken with the larger bulbs, the miniatures must be planted with care. Some plants produce a corm rather than a bulb, e.g. anemone and aconite, and corms should be planted no more than two inches deep; other depths may vary between three and four inches, depending upon the size of bulb and soil conditions. All bulbs should be planted an inch deeper in sandy than in heavy-textured soil. The following planting depths are suggested for any ordinary loamy soil:

Cyclamen coum „ *neapolitanum*	1 inch
Anemone species *Bulbocodium vernum* *Chionodoxa* *Colchicum* *Eranthis* *Iris reticulata* *Narcissus* species *Ranunculus* *Scilla sibirica*	2 inches
Allium moly and species *Corydalis* *Crocus* species *Erythronium dens-canis* *Hyacinthus amethystinus* *Leucojum vernum* *Muscari* species *Ornithogalum nutans* *Scilla nutans*	3 inches
Brodiaea grandiflora *Cyclamen europaeum* *Fritillaria meleagris* *Puschkinia scilloides* *Scilla Tubergeniana* *Sternbergia lutea* *Trillium* *Tulip* species	4 inches
Galanthus species *Lilium maculatum*	5 inches

Bulbs suitable for planting in a lawn:

Name	Flowering Time	Height
Chionodoxa gigantea	March–April	5 ins.
,, *luciliae*	March	4 ins.
,, *sardensis*	March	4 ins.
Crocus Balansae	March	1½ ins.
,, *biflorus*	March	3 ins.
,, *candidus*	April	2 ins.
,, *chrysanthus*	Feb.–April	4 ins.
,, *corsicus*	March	3 ins.
,, *Fleischeri*	Feb.–April	2 ins.
,, *imperati*	Jan.–March	3 ins.
,, *laevigatus*	Dec.–Feb.	3 ins.
,, *niveus*	Dec.–March	4 ins.
,, *Sieberi*	Feb.–March	3 ins.
,, *vernus*	March	2 ins.
Eranthis cilicica	Feb.–March	2 ins.
,, *hyemalis*	Jan.–March	2 ins.
Galanthus 'Colesbourne'	Feb.–March	4 ins.
,, *imperati*	Dec.–Jan.	6 ins.
,, *latifolius*	March–April	3 ins.
,, *nivalis*	Feb.–March	5 ins.
Iris Bakeriana	Jan.–Feb.	6 ins.
,, *Danfordiae*	February	4 ins.
,, *reticulata*	March–April	6 ins.
Narcissus bulbocodium	March–April	6 ins.
,, *cyclamineus*	March	9 ins.
,, *lobularis*	Feb.–March	8 ins.
,, *minimus*	Feb.–March	4 ins.
,, *nanus*	March–April	6 ins.
,, 'Rip van Winkle'	March	6 ins.
Scilla bifolia	Feb.–March	6 ins.
,, *sibirica*	Feb.–March	8 ins.
,, *Tubergeniana*	Feb.–March	5 ins.

The 'Emerald Velvet' lawn

Many more of the dwarf bulbs may be grown if one moves away from the traditional grass lawn and plants the Creeping Bent grass,

Agrostis stolonifera. When it was introduced about two years ago, there were many who were dubious about its qualities; but when I planted a small area in my garden with this 'grass', its ability to form and maintain a rich green carpet during the prolonged drought of 1959 amazed all who saw it. As such a 'lawn' will not require cutting until early June each year, the later-flowering spring bulbs may be planted, those which do not finish flowering until early May.

The bulbs are best planted before the 'lawn' is made, so as not to disturb the grass tufts, but if you plant later it is not difficult to part the tufts and plant in groups where space permits. The Creeping Bent grass grows at a much slower rate than ordinary lawn grass, and as the texture is more dense, like that of a tufted carpet, there will be less likelihood of cutting off the foliage too close before it has fully died back.

Agrostis stolonifera forms runners like a violet plant, the roots forming at the joints or nodes. A series of small tufts planted at intervals of ten to twelve square inches will quickly cover the whole area as runners form in all directions and quickly take root. The tufts are pulled apart almost like Couch grass or Mint roots, and the pieces being planted in a regular pattern with the aid of a garden line. If the plants are kept moist they will begin to grow at once and will completely cover the ground in about sixteen weeks from planting. The grass is surface rooting and forms clusters or clumps rather like a carpeting rock plant. Subsequent growth is considerably slower than that of ordinary lawn grasses and cutting every fortnight is all that is necessary. It does in fact spread laterally rather than shoot upwards, as is more usual. It will, however, smother almost all weeds; and, as may be expected from a lawn composed entirely of a single strain, is pleasing in appearance, as there are no variations of colour and leaf size. It cannot be cut as drastically as ordinary grass or bare patches will be revealed.

The strain marketed by Matt Templeton Ltd. of Grimsby is appropriately known as 'Emerald Velvet'. The planting method is as follows: First a shallow trench is made with a trowel, about an inch deep and four inches long and across the trench the offsets are placed with the ends just above soil level. These are left completely exposed while the trench is filled in with soil and made level with the surrounding ground. When the whole area has been planted in this way, the ground is rolled so that the stolons, or roots attached to the protruding offsets, will be pressed into the soil. All that is necessary now is to keep the plants moist and to remove any weeds until the plants begin to cover the ground. The lawn will benefit greatly from an annual dressing with lawn fertilizer, when once established; and as is the case with all lawns, the more it is walked upon the better it will become. In fact, where a lawn is frequently used a roller will not be necessary, and indeed may do more harm than good. An 'Emerald Velvet' lawn of a hundred square feet may be planted for 13s. 6d. The grass will grow well on almost all soils and in partial shade, but must not be allowed to invade the flower border, for it will run over the edges as rampantly as Buttercup or Strawberry. Continual edging of the lawn is therefore important, and long-arm shears should be used. Leaves should not be allowed to remain on the lawn a moment longer than necessary (this goes for all types of lawn), for a cover of wet leaves will cause the grass to decay.

A chamomile lawn

Miniature bulbs may also be planted among carpeting plants forming a colourful 'lawn' which will be entirely labour-saving and beautiful almost throughout the year.

As with the 'Emerald Velvet' Lawn, the herbs will tend to grow in an outward direction rather than upright, and quickly cover the ground, if planted about nine inches apart. They will require trimming only once or twice each summer. This may be done either with shears or with a mower which has the blades raised as high as possible. It was Falstaff who said of such a lawn, 'the more it is trodden upon, the faster it grows', and if your herb lawn is not walked upon at all often, it should be rolled as frequently as possible. The drier the soil the more fragrant will the plants be, and there are few more agreeable couches than a dry, sweet-smelling herb lawn on a hot day in summer.

If the soil is at all heavy, give it a dressing with caustic lime, and early in spring incorporate plenty of sand and grit. Planting may be done during April and for the first season, the lawn will have a rather sparse appearance. However, as soon as the plants become fully established they will form dense clumps completely covering the ground and will remain green and healthy for years with little attention.

At the end of the first summer, any unduly long shoots should be removed with the shears, but the plants will not require cutting with the mower. When established, cutting should be done only at the end of July and again possibly in autumn, for during the months of June and July the Thymes will be a mass of brilliant colour and the Chamomile flowers are always in demand for various purposes.

Anthemis nobilis is the carpeting Chamomile. Before the introduction of tobacco, its leaves were dried and used for smoking. But it is its white flowers that are of most value today. An ounce infused in a pint of boiling water makes a nerve tonic (a wineglassful is taken twice a day). The same preparation may be used as a hair tonic. Chamomile plants may be obtained for about 50*s*. per 100, though they may easily be raised from seed, a 2*s*. 6*d*. packet producing nearly a thousand plants. After planting, roll in the plants thoroughly where the soil is light and well drained. As with the 'Emerald Velvet' lawn, the plants should be weeded the first year; afterwards the plants will choke out all obnoxious weeds.

Plant with the Chamomile the creeping or prostrate Thymes, best planted from pots. All have tiny flower spikes and grey-green leaves. *Thymus serpyllum* is the creeping species, the form *coccineus* bearing deep purple-red flowers. A lovely variety is 'Annie Hall', which forms mats of flesh-pink flowers; 'Pink Chintz' has flowers of a good shade of salmon-pink. With *T. coccineus* plant the variety *alba*, or 'Snowdrift', both white-flowered. Another creeping thyme is *T. lanuginosus*, its silvery leaves, as the name implies, of woolly appearance. Also interesting is *T. micans*, forming grey-green mats studded with mauve, and of pine-like scent. *T. odoratus* also is particularly aromatic.

The Creeping Mints are useful in the herbal lawn. *Mentha pulegium* literally hugs the ground, and *M. requienii* forms a thick mat studded with tiny mauve flowers. Both emit a powerful fragrance when trodden upon. Another plant of creeping form is the *Calamintha* or Basil Thyme and leaves and blue flowers emit a strong minty odour. The uncommon *Micromeria corsica*, of heavy incense-perfume, should be included in a lawn of herb plants. It is like a tiny heather with grey foliage and pretty purple flowers. Another plant of mat-like habit is the Mountain Vetch, *Anthyllis montana*, a member of the Pea family, which bears scented red Clover-like blooms. All these interesting plants may be planted together though the Chamomile should preponderate, for it is inexpensive, extremely tough, and remains pleasantly green throughout the year whatever the weather.

The bulbs should be set out between the plants through which they will grow as the carpeters begin to spread. As cutting will be done only with shears, bulbs to bloom throughout the year may be grown, omitting those growing less than three inches tall or more than nine. The Chamomile may be clipped around any bulbs still in bloom or those making growth and which will flower during autumn. In any case, as with the 'Emerald Velvet' lawn, no clipping will be necessary until the end of June.

Bulbs for the waterside

Those who have a pond or stream in their garden should make lavish use of a number of bulbous plants for planting along the banks in rough grass which should be cut short in autumn. The bulbs may be planted in groups, and where the grass is removed in places, use should be made of Azaleas and other spring-flowering plants which appreciate a moist position. The Spiraeas and Astilbes are good choices here, and groups of *Primula rosea* and P. *denticulata* in some of their numerous varieties should be planted between the groups of bulbs.

Where the grass can be kept short, drifts of Winter Aconites may be planted, for this bulbous plant is the earliest bloomer of those which are tolerant of moisture. The dainty Cyclamen-flowered Daffodil, *Narcissus cyclamineus*, is also happy in a moist soil, the clear yellow flowers with reflexed perianth being borne on eight-inch stems. It thrives best in a moist soil containing some sand and peat; where the soil is too heavy, the tiny bulbs may decay.

Fritillaria meleagris is happy by the waterside and is to be found growing naturally about water-meadows in the Thames valley. But since excessive moisture may lead to decay, it is wise to plant on a layer of sand. *F. citrina* will be long-living if planted close to water, provided that the soil is well-drained.

Drifts of *Anemone nemorosa* may be planted by water, particularly where it is possible to provide shade also. The variety 'Royal Blue' mingles well with the white-flowering. *Hyacinthus amethystinus* is tolerant of moisture and should be planted in groups close to *Primula rosea*, which will come into bloom at the same time.

CHAPTER 4

Bulbs in the Shrubbery

*Conditions of a shrubbery—Plants and bulbs for a lime-laden soil—
Bulbs for a sun-baked soil—Plants and bulbs for an acid soil—Care of
the shrubbery*

Flowering trees and shrubs have generally a short flowering season, so that for long periods they offer little but foliage. Miniature bulbs planted beneath them will, however, provide a carpet of colour throughout the year. Here may also be grown most of those less hardy plants which in the company of low-growing shrubs and heathers will receive the protection they require where planted in the more exposed parts of the country.

Conditions of a shrubbery

The shrubbery may be an alternative to the semi-wild garden; though whereas in the woodland garden the bulbs will be shaded, and the soil moist and leafy, in most shrubberies entirely opposite conditions will prevail. Ornamental trees may be used to give privacy and they should be planted at the back of the shrubbery. To the front evergreen and deciduous shrubs combine to provide as long a period of colour as possible, whether of flowers, berries or foliage. In front of the shrubs, groups of Heathers should be planted in suitable soils, and among these the less hardy bulbs may be set. Winter-flowering Heathers will give ground colour to a shrubbery from Christmas until early spring, at the same time protecting from cold winds those bulbs which will come into bloom during spring and early summer.

Such bulbs as will flourish under dry and poor soil conditions should be planted in the shrubbery, as well as those whose foliage tends to become coarse and untidy after flowering (e.g., the colchicums), and which will benefit from being partially hidden by the shrubs.

40

BULBS IN THE SHRUBBERY

As the shrubbery will be left undisturbed for several years, the soil should be thoroughly cleaned of all perennial weeds and enriched with humus-forming materials before any planting is done. Liberal quantities of plant food should be incorporated, for it must be remembered that both shrubs and bulbs will be expected to flourish with but little attention for some considerable time. As they become established the bulbs will increase rapidly and will quickly cover the ground, choking out any weeds, but at the same time making it almost impossible to work the soil.

The soil of a town garden shrubbery will often be of an acid nature thanks to constant deposits of soot and sulphur, and where lime is not naturally present, this should be incorporated before any bulbs are introduced.

Plants and bulbs for a lime-laden soil

There are quite a number of bulbs which will tolerate heavy quantities of lime in the soil but among Heathers, only varieties of *Erica carnea* will prove to be lime-tolerant. These are the Winter-flowering Heathers. The first comes into bloom in November and it is possible, by planting numerous varieties, to provide colour until the end of April. Being evergreen, the foliage will give adequate protection to the less hardy of the summer-flowering bulbs, at a time when the Heathers are not in bloom.

The Winter-flowering Heathers grow between six and eight inches tall and will quickly make clumps eighteen inches in diameter. Outstanding is the new variety, 'Eileen Porter', which actually comes into bloom towards the end of October and continues to bear its rich carmine flowers until mid-April. It remains in bloom longer than any other Heather. For bloom during the mid-winter months, *E. praecox rubra* has dark green foliage and flowered spikes of richest crimson; 'Queen Mary' has bright pink flowers and prefers lime in its diet; and *Calluna vulgaris aurea*, with golden foliage and bright, deep-pink flowers, is attractive. For spring flowering, plant *E. 'Vivellii'* which has bronze leaves and carmine-red flower spikes, and the 'Springwoods', white and pink, of almost prostrate habit.

In a chalky soil may be grown: all members of the Prunus family, the Flowering Almonds and Cherries; the Philadelphus or Mock Orange; Flowering Currants; Forsythia and Flowering Quince; Buddleias, Weigelas and Lilacs. Here, too, may be planted (with the

41

winter-flowering heathers to provide ground cover) the Rock-roses and Dwarf Barberries. Like plants tolerant of lime, they also flourish in a dry, sun-baked soil, and like the heather, they are evergreen and provide valuable protection for the bulbs.

Of the dwarf Rock-roses, *Cistus corbariensis* is one of the hardiest, growing only two feet tall and bearing pure white flowers throughout midsummer. Of the barberries, *Berberis chrysosphaera* makes a low, broad bush eighteen inches high and has dark, shiny leaves and lemon-yellow flowers. Growing to a similar height is *B. buxifolia nana*, which forms a graceful little bush with dark, Box-like foliage.

Among the most suitable bulbs for a lime-laden soil are the Anemones: not just the Poppy anemones grown in large numbers for cutting but the many lovely species which quickly form a carpet of rich colouring and are cheap enough to buy in quantity. They are not bulbs, strictly speaking, but tubers. Though their name is derived from the Greek *anemos*, meaning Wind (Flower), they detest strong winds and for this reason are happiest in the shelter of a shrubbery. Have them growing in drifts beneath the golden bells of the Forsythia, which will be in bloom at the same time and will act as foil for the brilliant blue flowers of *A. blanda* and A. *apennina*. Plant with them Miniature daffodils of taller habit than most, such as the golden-flowered 'W. P. Milner', for which the Anemones will in their turn provide a carpet of blue as foil.

As soon as the snow has gone from our gardens, *Anemone apennina* shows its fern-like foliage; later, in early April, its bright blue flowers with golden centre appear on six-inch stems. Equally beautiful is the Grecian Windflower, *A. blanda*, which will flourish in a chalk hollow beneath young trees, or in the shrubbery at the foot of silver-birch trees. It bears flowers of deepest blue on four-inch stems in early spring; equally attractive is the variety *rosea*, with flowers of delicate rose-pink.

Useful with the anemones are the Wood Sorrels which are rarely planted in our gardens because they seed themselves and increase their bulblets with such rapidity that they tend to become a nuisance. In the shrubbery, however, their vigour is in their favour, for their Clover-like foliage, often tinted with purple, is of a good fresh green. Not all the Wood Sorrels like the shady conditions which suit our native *Oxalis acetosalla*, for the best species are natives of South Africa and South America and enjoy a warm, dry border and a soil containing some lime. *O. Bowieana*, under such conditions, bears umbels of rose-coloured flowers right through summer, and *O. adenophylla* lifts its rosy cups on three-inch stems above attractive grey foliage.

Also of vigorous habit, and best confined to the shrubbery, is the handsome Golden Garlic, *Allium moly*, having bright yellow heads on twelve-inch stems during early summer; it provides a welcome glow of colour in the shadowy nooks of a shrubbery. It will grow almost anywhere and in any type of soil, especially one containing some lime. Parkinson tells us that John Tradescant, who achieved fame at the beginning of the seventeenth century as a collector of new plants for the Duke of Buckingham, grew this *Allium* in his garden near Canterbury; and adds, 'It was he who sent me a root to plant in my garden' (now Long Acre, in London). The two great gardeners must have been firm friends for in the year (1629) of the publication of the *Paradisus*, Parkinson was appointed botanist to Charles I and Tradescant head gardener to the King.

'Sweet is moly, but its root is ill'

wrote the poet Spenser, who knew of the delicacy of its bloom and the pungency of its root. Gerard, writing at the same time, called the Moly a 'stately' plant.

With *A. moly* plant *A. ursinum*, which grows to a similar height and bears handsome heads of fragrant mealy white flowers during June. There are many other choice flowering Garlics for the shrubbery, such as *A. flavum* and *A. pulchellum*, the latter with violet-pink flowers in August; but they grow rather too tall to be classed as 'miniature' bulbs. For all that they should be included where space permits, since they are extremely hardy and among the most inexpensive of bulbs.

Nor, where the soil is dry and sun-baked and has a high lime content, should the Dwarf Irises be omitted. *Iris reticulata* in its numerous forms may be planted, but, though expensive, do not neglect *I. Bakeriana*, hardier even than *I. reticulata* and coming into bloom with the New Year. The standards are 'shot' with mauve, and the violet fall petals have a large white blotch, studded with black spots. It is similar to *Iris histrioides*, which blooms at the same time.

The Miniature daffodils will also grow in a lime-laden soil, though not for choice. They are in habit excellent plants for a shrubbery, where their foliage may be left undisturbed to die back completely, hidden by low-growing shrubs. Plant in clumps or circles of half a dozen bulbs, preferably near the Irises and Anemones for colour contrast.

N. lobularis is a dainty little Daffodil, its flower having a perianth of pale yellow with a deeper yellow trumpet. *N. juncifolius*, the miniature Rush-leaf Daffodil, is most tolerant of lime. It bears fragrant flowers like those of the Jonquil and should be planted near the edges of a shrubbery. *N. cernuus*, with its nodding flowers of silvery white, grows to a height of ten to twelve inches. It is delightful in the shrubbery, as is Queen Anne's Double Daffodil, *N. capax plenus*. All will appreciate some leaf mould placed about the bulbs at planting time.

The *Chionodoxa*, *Puschkinia* and *Galanthus* species will also grow well in a soil containing lime, but like the Narcissus they will grow even better in a neutral soil, for these bulbs do like a soil enriched with humus.

Bulbs for a lime-laden soil:

Name	Flowering Time	Height
Allium anceps	August	6 ins.
„ *karataviense*	May	10 ins.
„ *moly*	June	12 ins.
„ *ursinum*	April	12 ins.
Anemone apennina	March–April	6 ins.
„ *blanda*	March–April	3–4 ins.
Chionodoxa gigantea	April	5 ins.
„ *luciliae*	March–April	4 ins.
Cyclamen Atkinsii	Dec.–March	4 ins.
„ *graecum*	July–Sept.	6 ins.
„ *libanoticum*	March–April	6 ins.
„ *neapolitanum*	Sept.–Nov.	4 ins.
„ *repandum*	April–May	6 ins.
Galanthus imperati	Dec.–Jan.	6 ins.
„ *Olgae*	Oct.–Nov.	6 ins.
„ *plicatus*	March	8 ins.
Iris Bakeriana	Jan.–Feb.	6 ins.
„ *histrioides*	March	6 ins.
„ *reticulata*	March–April	6 ins.
Narcissus cernuus	April	9 ins.
„ *juncifolius*	April	4 ins.
„ *lobularis*	Feb.–March	8 ins.
„ *odorus*	May	8 ins.

BULBS IN THE SHRUBBERY

Name	Flowering Time	Height
Narcissus triandrus	April	6 ins.
Oxalis adenophylla	May–June	3 ins.
,, *Bowieana*	June–July	9 ins.
Puschkinia scilloides	March–May	4 ins.

Bulbs for a sun-baked soil

In a shrubbery where the soil tends to be dry and sun-baked but is neither too acid nor too alkaline, try the Grape Hyacinths, with tiny grape-like blooms massed together on short stems like miniature Hyacinths. The botanical name, *Muscari*, is derived from its old name, *Hyacinthus moschatum*, the Musk Hyacinth, its rather dingy yellowish-purple blooms having a pronounced perfume of musk. Though natives of Mediterranean shores, all the Muscari are extremely hardy; the smaller are suitable for the rockery, and all are attractive for growing in small pots. In the shrubbery or border they increase rapidly from seed and by means of offsets, so do not plant more closely than six inches apart.

Interesting rather than beautiful is the Plume Hyacinth, *Muscari comosum monstrosum*, which bears its flowers on twelve-inch spikes. The lower flowers, which are fertile, are of greenish-purple, and above these the brilliant blue filaments which are infertile flowers produce a plume-like effect. Excellent for cutting, for mixing with late spring flowers, it blooms in May. A recent introduction from Persia, and in bloom in April, is *M. Tubergenianum* or the 'Oxford and Cambridge Hyacinth', its 'grapes' opening pale blue and changing to dark blue with age. But for massing there are no more striking flowers than those wonderful hybrids 'Cantab' and 'Heavenly Blue', both of which are fragrant, their dainty spikes of tiny globular bells lasting throughout April and into May, acting as a charming contrast to the Miniature daffodils. Their prostrate leaves cover the ground and thus protect the flower-spikes from soil splashing. *M. neglectum* is also excellent for naturalising. It is free flowering and does well anywhere, its spikes of blue-black 'grapes' appearing above pale green foliage.

For a sunny shrubbery, the Spring Meadow Saffron, *Bulbocodium vernum*, is a delightful plant. It bears its Colchicum-like blooms on four-inch stems in early spring before its leaves. They are lavender-pink, and take on a star-like form as they open. It likes some sun and a dry soil so plant it to the front of a shrubbery where its rather coarse leaves will be hidden by dwarf shrubby plants as they die back.

The *Bulbocodium* blooms in spring, *Sternbergia lutea*, the Lily of the Fields, in autumn. The latter bears a large crocus-like bloom of glistening yellow above rich green strap-like leaves. Both take a year to become established, but are well worth waiting for. They revel in sun-baked conditions and are such choice plants that one would like to see them more often. The *Sternbergia* will grow well in a lime-laden soil.

Having foliage of the same coarse habit, the Colchicums or Autumn Crocuses should join the *Bulbocodium* and *Sternbergia* in the shrubbery, for they are not suitable for growing elsewhere. The new hybrids are quite outstanding plants, with flowers like those of the huge Dutch spring-flowering Crocuses; like the species, they bloom from early September until the beginning of December, long after their coarse strap-like foliage has disappeared. 'Naked Ladies' was their old country name. Be sure to plant that most striking species, *C. Bornmuelleri*, the first to bloom. Its huge lilac-rose flowers have a striking silvery centre. Plant for succession, so that the shrubbery will remain bright throughout autumn. The last to bloom is *C. autumnale* (purple) and its pure white counterpart, *album*. Planted with them, the autumn flowering Crocuses will provide additional colour in the shrubbery during dull November days. At one time the plants were to be found growing in the apple orchards of Somerset.

In a sheltered shrubbery in full sun, and where the hardy Heathers are used to give protection, most of the less hardy bulbs, chiefly those native to South Africa, may be grown. The handsome Red Cape Lilies, the *Tritonia*, the *Sparaxis* and the closely related *Streptanthera* will survive if given winter protection, but as they are such striking plants they merit cool house culture, and so are described in Chapter 11. If used about the shrubbery, they should be kept away from bulbs of vigorous habit. As most of the bulbous plants from warm climates bear their flowers on rather thin, wiry stems, they will receive support from the Heathers, and so should be planted as close to them as possible, in the same way that outdoor freesias are grown. The *Babiana* and *Calochortus* will not tolerate lime.

For a sun-baked soil, but preferably one in which leaf mould or humus in some other form has been incorporated, the *Brodiaeas* are outstanding plants. They will not find the presence of lime a drawback, if the humus is there too. As natives of California, they will appreciate the protection provided by Heathers and other low-growing shrubs. They bloom from mid-May until mid-July, when the great flush of spring-flowering bulbs is ending.

First to bloom is *Brodiaea crocea*, with umbels of yellow flowers on six- to eight-inch stems showing before the end of May. Then comes *B. grandiflora*, with deep blue flowers during June. Perhaps the best, and certainly the most striking, is the 'Californian Firecracker', *B. coccinea*; its pendulous flowers are brilliant crimson, tipped with green, and are borne during June and July on twelve-inch stems.

The Crocus species, planted in drifts, will grow well in a dry soil and a sunny position. The winter and early spring-flowering species in particular will enjoy the protection afforded by low-growing shrubby plants.

Bulbs for a sun-baked soil:

Name	*Flowering Time*	*Height*
Brodiaea coccinea	June–July	12 ins.
„ *crocea*	May–June	6 ins.
„ *grandiflora*	June	8 ins.
„ *ixioides*	May–June	9 ins.
„ *multiflora*	June–July	9 ins.
Bulbocodium vernum	March	3 ins.
Colchicum agrippinum	Sept.–Oct.	4–5 ins.
„ *autumnale*	Oct.–Nov.	6 ins.
„ *Bornmuelleri*	Aug.–Sept.	8 ins.
„ *byzantinum*	Aug.–Oct.	6 ins.
„ *callicymbium*	Sept.–Oct.	6 ins.
„ *luteum*	April	3 ins.
„ *speciosum*	Aug.–Nov.	9 ins.
Crocus species	Sept.–April	2–4 ins.
Muscari comosum	April–May	12 ins.
„ *conicum*	April	8 ins.
„ *moschatum*	March–April	6 ins.
„ *neglectum*	April–May	6 ins.
„ *plumosum*	May	9 ins.
„ *Tubergenianum*	April–June	9 ins.
Sternbergia Fischeriana	Feb.–March	9 ins.
„ *lutea*	Sept.–Oct.	8 ins.
Tulipa Batalini	April	4 ins.
„ *Eichleri*	April	12 ins.

BULBS IN THE SHRUBBERY

Name	Flowering Time	Height
Tulipa Fosteriana	April	8 ins.
,, *Greigii*	April	9 ins.
,, *Kaufmanniana*	March–April	8–9 ins.
,, *Kolpakowskiana*	April	9 ins.

Plants and bulbs for an acid soil

An acid soil may be brought into a more neutral condition by the addition of quantities of lime rubble, but there are still numerous plants and bulbs which will grow well in an acid soil. The most important are those of the Rhododendron group, which includes the Azaleas.

For early-spring blooming, the Japanese azaleas, with neat Box-like foliage, and growing only fifteen to eighteen inches tall, are most suitable for a small garden. Slightly taller are the *A. malvatica* hybrids, also evergreen, their foliage taking on brilliant autumnal hues. One of the loveliest is 'Fedora', with dusky pink flowers, and 'Blaauws Pink' bears hose-in-hose flowers of rich salmon-pink. The *A. mollis* hybrids bloom in May. They are not evergreen and grow tall and bushy.

Next in importance are the Heathers, with one or two exceptions enjoying a peaty soil. *E. cinerea atro-rubens*, summer-flowering, has ruby-red flowers on stems of only six inches. It should be planted to the front of a shrubbery, and for contrast plant *alba minor*, for abundant white flowers.

The Dorset heath, *E. ciliaris*, makes a compact plant two feet high, and in summer bears spikes of clear pink; 'Mrs. C. H. Gill' has cerise flowers and dark green foliage. For contrast, plant *Calluna aurea* with its golden foliage.

Varieties of *Calluna* (*Erica*) *vulgaris* will bloom throughout autumn and among the best are *aurea*, with purple flowers and golden foliage turning bronze in winter; and *cuprea*, its copper-coloured foliage turning crimson in winter. There are many more lovely Heathers; a whole border could be planted with them to give colour the whole year round.

The Daphnes will also grow well in a peaty soil, as will the Pieris or Lily-of-the-Valley bush, and the Kalmias. Of the more vigorous shrubs both the Arbutus and Magnolia flourish in such conditions.

For planting in the shade of tall trees as well as in the shrubbery,

48

12. *Oxalis adenophylla*

13. *Iris reticulata* 'Cantab'

14. *Iris Bakeriana.* A beautiful Dwarf Iris. Ideal as a pot plant or for the alpine garden

15. *Iris Danfordiae.* Showing orchid-like bloom: a clear lemon yellow with beautiful dark green spots in the throat

A. nemorosa, the Wood Anemone, is an exquisite plant. Like *A. vernalis*, it will not tolerate lime. It is native to our shady woodlands and if used in the shrubbery should be planted in pockets of peat or leaf mould. The best form is *Robinsoniana*, with large flowers of a pale lavender colour with golden anthers. Of this variety, the Rev. Harpur Crewe said, 'All fade before its simple and innocent loveliness'. The variety 'Royal Blue' should also be planted for its deep blue flowers. There is also a double white form, *flore pleno*.

Anemone sylvestris, the Snowdrop anemone, also likes a peaty soil. Its nodding snow-white flowers bloom in June with the later flowering scillas, which also do well in an acid soil. *A. s. amethystina*, perhaps the best of these, bears large spikes of clearest blue on six-inch stems.

An early writer holds that 'for their beauty as well as for the earliness of their blooms, the Winter Aconites are deserving of a prime place in our gardens'. They like a moist, peaty soil, but will grow well anywhere. Most gardeners know *Eranthis hyemalis*, the old Winter Aconite, which covers the ground with its bright emerald green foliage long after its yellow cups have died away. Few seem to know *E. cilicica*, from Asia Minor. It is a little more expensive but its flowers are larger, and the foliage, more delicately cut, is tinted with bronze. Both should be grown, for *E. cilicica* comes into bloom when *E. hyemalis* has finished flowering.

For those who would wish to have a quite outstanding plant in the garden, the new *Eranthis* 'Guinea Gold' is truly beautiful, but as yet expensive. It is the result of a cross between *E. hyemalis* and *E. cilicica*, and has the bronzy foliage of the latter and a huge cup-shaped bloom of delicious perfume. Just one or two planted together will brighten the darkest corner of a garden. They hold their blooms full face to the winter sunshine. Even a fall of snow will have little effect on their hardiness; the flowers will still be shining bright as soon as a thaw sets in and they emerge from their covering.

Another bulbous plant which will grow in a peaty soil is the *Corydalis*. I used to grow it on a sunny rockery with complete lack of success until I discovered that the plants were native of the woodlands of Russia and Northern Europe, and though liking a well-drained soil do best in partial shade. Not all are bulbous plants. *C. cava* (for the shrubbery), so called because of its curiously hollow bulb, is a charming plant, bearing, during April and May, pale lilac blooms on nine-inch stems above attractive grey foliage. Of similar habit and in bloom at the same time is *C. angustifolia*, with loose sprays of pale

D 49

pink flowers. Its dwarf counterpart, *C. solida*, seems to be rather easier to grow.

Bulbs which will grow in an Acid soil:

Name	Flowering Time	Height
Anemone nemorosa	April–June	6 ins.
„ *sylvestris*	May–June	12 ins.
Corydalis cava	April–May	8 ins.
„ *decipiens*	May	9 ins.
„ *densiflora*	March–April	6 ins.
„ *Wilsonii*	April–May	8 ins.
Eranthis cilicica	Feb.–March	2 ins.
„ *hyemalis*	Jan.–Feb.	2 ins.
Scilla amethystina	May–June	8 ins.
„ *pratensis*	May–June	7 ins.

Care of the shrubbery

Before any planting of bulbs, the ground should be brought into as suitable a condition as possible. Ground which has been planted with shrubs for some considerable time will have become exhausted, and as much humus as can be obtained should be worked in before the bulbs are planted in autumn. Material from the garden compost heap, old mushroom bed compost, peat and leaf mould, bark fibre and used hops are all suitable for digging into the soil around the shrubs, which will obtain considerable benefit from their new diet.

Also, if the shrubbery has been long established, a number of the plants may have made excessive growth, causing overcrowding and depriving nearby plants and the ground beneath them of sunlight and air. They should be cut back at the appropriate time, taking into consideration the natural habit of the plants. To prevent overcrowding, it may be advisable to remove one or two of the most vigorous plants altogether, possibly replacing by one or two of more compact habit.

The bulbs should be planted in generous groups, placing those of taller habit behind the low-growing shrubs such as the Heathers and Rock-roses. Space out the plantings so that there will be splashes of colour throughout the shrubbery at all times of the year.

If the ground has been well prepared before planting, all that will be necessary will be to give a liberal mulching when the dead foliage of the bulbs is removed in autumn and when the shrubs are trimmed, any dead or decayed wood being removed at the same time. There will be no need to fork over the ground, for this would cause disturbance and perhaps damage to the bulbs. A regular mulch will enable the shrubs to form plenty of vigorous new wood and will also keep the bulbs supplied with valuable humus and plant food. They will multiply rapidly and yet remain free-flowering for many years without lifting and dividing. In fact, the shrubbery carpeted with bulbs could become the most colourful and labour-saving part of the garden.

CHAPTER 5

A Border of Miniature Bulbs

Size of the border—Preparing the border—Planting—Bulbs to plant in early summer—Bulbs to plant in autumn

A border of herbaceous plants can give colour during all but the mid-winter months; one of miniature bulbs will provide colour throughout the year, and there will be no need for tying and staking. Such a border will be permanent and will give more colour for the ground occupied than any other plants. The border may be of any length and in any part of the garden except where sunshine is almost completely excluded. It should not be too wide, or the dainty habit of the small bulbous flowering plants will cause them to be overlooked. From two to three feet, depending on length, will be sufficient. A most attractive background is a wattle hurdle fence, much less tedious to maintain than the all-too-common privet hedge.

In my own garden the miniature border is close to a small plantation of ornamental trees, now about five feet high. A low hedge of the evergreen *Senecio Greyii* separates the border from the coppice, which is planted with suitable bulbs to provide a long period of colour. The border is forty feet in length and nearly three feet wide, and faces the house, so that the beauty of the flowers may be enjoyed to the full during almost all the year. Bulbs from the original planting have multiplied vigorously, but as they show no signs of exhausting the soil they are left undisturbed, and receive no attention other than a yearly mulch given in July. At this time, most of the plants will be dying back, and those which bloom during autumn and through winter will not have begun to make much growth.

A yearly mulch is essential for maintaining the vigour of the bulbs. One containing plant food will replace that which has been removed from the soil, and will help to retain moisture in the soil during summer, will provide winter protection for the small bulbs, and will help to suppress annual weeds. A yearly mulch obviates weeding,

52

apart from the removal of an occasional perennial weed. This means that bulbs are not unduly disturbed. With bulbs, there is none of the constant labour exacted by bedding plants. Once planted the bulbs may be left undisturbed for years if necessary, or if they become overcrowded they may be lifted and divided as opportunity presents itself.

The ideal mulch for increasing humus content and improving soil texture is one consisting of moist peat, riddled turf loam and decayed manure (preferably cow manure) in equal parts. The bulbs will revel in it, increasing rapidly and remaining vigorous and free flowering without attention for many years. An equally satisfactory mulch mixture is of moist peat, mixed with old mushroom bed compost or decayed turf loam to which has been added a quantity of decayed manure (say, one part to two parts of soil), with peat predominating. Spread to a depth of at least an inch. Anything less will fail to suppress weeds.

Where possible, give a mulch during early July, taking care not to damage late summer- and autumn-flowering bulbs making new growth, and another towards the year's end. Where annuals are to be grown between the bulbs, then one thick mulch only should be given, in December when the border is tidied.

Preparing the border

Bulbs enjoy a soil moist in summer and well drained in winter. A light, sandy soil may be made more moisture-retentive by incorporating humus in the form of peat, leaf mould, shoddy, decayed manure, bark fibre, used hops or material from the compost heap, whichever is most readily obtainable. Even the smallest bulbs are deeply rooting and so the humus and plant food should be worked well into the soil. Lucky is he (or she) who enjoys a friable, loamy soil in which to garden, for apart from a limited application of humus in the form of plant food, such as decayed manure, hops or old mushroom bed compost, the ground will require no other attention.

A heavy soil, of a high clay content, so often found in town gardens and particularly that of newly built property, must be made as friable as possible before any bulbs are planted, otherwise they will decay through excess moisture remaining about the roots for long periods while the bulbs are dormant and there is little root action to utilize the moisture. Drainage materials in the form of boiler ash, grit or coarse sand should first be incorporated as the ground is being cleared of perennial weeds. Crushed bricks may also be added. Most important, leave the soil in a lumpy condition to enable the frosts and winds of winter to pulverize it. The humus materials may next be incorporated. Where there is much clay, treat with caustic (unhydrated) lime during autumn or early winter when the drainage materials are being dug in. The preparation Krilium is proving efficient in breaking up a heavy soil. It is applied in powder form, sprinkled over the surface, but will prove of value only if used when the soil is dry. It will render a wet clay soil even more sticky.

If the soil is left to the elements during winter, the final preparations may be completed early in spring when the autumn and early winter flowering bulbs may be planted. If you wish to plant the border without undue delay, prepare it during September and plant with spring flowering bulbs while there is still time for the bulbs to become established before the severe weather. This will be possible only where the soil is light and friable.

Planting

A border of bulbs should be planted in exactly the same way as a herbaceous border, with bulbs of slightly taller habit at the back, and some 'staggering' to ensure that there are never unduly large areas devoid of colour for any length of time. The autumn and early winter flowering plants should be planted in groups between those which bloom during spring and early summer. Do not plant in one's and two's, but make a bold planting of each species or variety so that the full beauty of each may be enjoyed. First mark out the border into numerous sections using dry sand or sawdust, each section large enough to accommodate six bulbs spaced 3 inches apart. To facilitate planting and ordering, each section should be marked with a small wooden label on which is written the name of the species or variety. The labels may be moved about the border until the grouping is such that the whole border will be colourful over as long a period as possible.

Do not plant too closely, but remember that the miniature bulbs, with few exceptions, make little leaf. The bulbs should not be planted too formally, for through over-rigidity the natural charm of the plants will be lost. As with naturalising (Chapter 2) use long-lived species so that replacements will be few and far between. As an example, the

Tulip species should be preferred to the Dutch varieties which are generally used for bedding.

Depth of planting will be governed by the condition of the soil. As a general rule, do not plant the tiny bulbs more than two inches below the surface of the ground in heavy soil, but where the soil is light and friable, plant an inch deeper (see Chapter 2). Where the soil is heavy, to remove a two-inch layer from each section and plant the bulbs on a layer of peat and sand to ensure adequate drainage. Peat may be packed around the bulbs before they are covered with soil. Never plant when the soil is too wet and do not tread unduly, for an over-compact soil mass is short of both oxygen and soil organisms.

Plants which tend to reproduce themselves rather too liberally, e.g. the Windflowers and the Wood Sorrels, should be excluded from the bulb border, as should the true dwarfs, which will come into their own in the rockery, in window boxes and in troughs. If your bulb border is north of the Thames, bulbs of more tender habit should be omitted, especially where the soil is heavy; though if heathers are used for additional winter colour these tender subjects may be used, as the heathers will protect them.

One is often asked which is the best method of concealing the foliage which is dying back, and which is always unsightly at this time. My own practice is never to remove any foliage until the border is tidied in winter. It is then raked up and burnt before a mulch is given.

It is a good idea to plant bulbs which bloom early behind those which bloom later. Various species of Hardy Cyclamen also give pleasing coverage, for their foliage remains colourful for a long period, and gives useful protection from strong sunlight.

Shrubby plants may be dotted about the border to hide the dying foliage. Quite excellent in this respect is *Berberis Bristolensis*, making a low bush two feet wide of glossy evergreen foliage. It will provide valuable shelter for winter-flowering bulbs. Equally good is *B. buxifolia nana*, also evergreen, with neat, box-like leaves. The evergreen Rock-roses, especially *Cistus algarvensis*, and such dwarf heathers as are tolerant of some lime in the soil, may also be used.

As an alternative, why not sow annuals which grow only an inch or so tall around the clumps of bulbs, where they are to bloom, during spring? The Rock Pimpernel, *Anagallis linifolia 'Phillipsii'*, will quickly cover the ground with its Gentian-blue flowers, and the

Violet Cress plant, *Ionopsidium acaule*, bears white flowers, tinged with violet, right through summer. Equally useful is *Linaria maroccana*, 'Fairy Bouquet' with richly coloured Antirrhinum-like flowers on four- to five-inch stems. The Californian Bluebell, *Phacelia campanularia*, forms a dense carpet spangled with tiny bells of navy-blue. All these plants will flower until the autumn but may be left to provide green until they are removed, together with the dead foliage of the bulbs, in winter.

Bulbs to plant in early summer

For spring planting in a suitably prepared soil, one of the loveliest border plants is the Zephyr Flower, and possibly the best species is *Zephyranthes candida*, with evergreen foliage and a profusion of white Crocus-like flowers on eight- to nine-inch stems throughout early autumn. The species *Z. carinata* has flowers of soft rose-red with striking golden anthers, blooms at the same time, and grows to a similar height. Plant at the middle of the border and behind it the attractive Japanese lily, *L. maculatum*, the smallest lily known (growing less than twelve inches tall) and the only one to be mentioned in this book. It is stem rooting and so should be planted five to six inches deep, preferably in a light soil. The flowers are cup-shaped, three or four to a stem, blooming during mid-summer. The bulbs should be planted on sand. There are several lovely forms; 'Alice Wilson', lemon-yellow; 'Kikat', apricot-coloured spotted with black.

The Miniature gladiolus, *G. nanus*, bears its flower spike on a twelve-inch stem during July. It is a most decorative border plant but as it may not be quite hardy in the North it should be covered with ashes each winter. Unlike the large-flowered Gladioli, it does not require lifting each year; the corms remain healthy for many years in a well-drained soil, where they will multiply rapidly. Plant it, if possible, among dwarf heathers for protection and support.

In July plant the autumn- and early winter-flowering Crocuses, and that quite distinct race of autumn-flowering plants, the Colchicums, with Crocus-like flowers. Though the large-flowered Dutch hybrid Crocuses are planted by the million each autumn to bloom in spring, the equally handsome autumn-flowering species is almost entirely neglected. They provide rich colour when few other bulbs are in bloom.

The earliest is *C. zonatus*, with rosy-lilac trumpet, then follows

C. pulchellus, of pale lavender bloom with an orange throat; both will be in bloom during September. For October plant the striped *C. asturicus* and that finest of all Crocuses, *C. medius*, whose rich violet trumpet and red stigmas provide a brilliant note of colour as the autumn days shorten. As October wanes, the Saffron crocus, *C. sativus*, comes into bloom, its lilac flowers feathered with violet. Cheap enough to buy, it blooms freely, once established. In a sunny, sheltered border the dainty *C. laevigatus Fontenayi* will offer its attractive lilac and buff flowers almost up to Christmas when *C. imperati*, also fragrant and of similar colouring, takes over, to be followed by *C. Korolkowi*, brilliant gold, and *C. Sieberi*, lavender-blue. The late winter-flowering species should be planted with the spring-blooming, during October. In March will appear *C. chrysanthus* and its numerous lovely hybrid varieties; *C. Tomasinianus* with its long, pencil-like trumpets, and *C. vernus*, to be followed by the colourful Dutch hybrids in April. Each of these Crocuses should be planted liberally in groups all over the border.

The Colchicums come into bloom before the foliage appears. This foliage is coarse and large, so the Colchicums, if not confined to the shrubbery, should be allowed more room in the border than the Crocuses. They are considerably more expensive, costing anything above 2s. 0d. each, but are also extremely long lasting. *C. speciosum* has a most handsome bloom of velvet-like appearance and of brilliant carmine colouring. It is the first to flower. For October, *C. autumnale album*, with glistening white flowers, and the new hybrid, 'Rosy Dawn', are the most beautiful.

The Snake's Head Fritillaries, most popular for naturalising, are also colourful additions to a border which is, after all, something of a compromise between naturalising and bedding, combining the attractive qualities of both. *F. meleagris* 'Aphrodite' with large, graceful, pure white blooms in May on nine- to twelve-inch stems, is perhaps the most showy.

Also May-flowering are the dwarf Alliums, which should be planted with plenty of room at the back of the border, *A. moly*, the Golden Garlic, makes rather rampant growth and is best confined to the shrubbery. *A. karataviense*, a native of Turkestan, has globular heads of reddish-mauve; to the front of the border plant *A. ostrowskianum*, having rosy heads on six-inch stems throughout June; it is a plant of neat, compact habit.

A BORDER OF MINIATURE BULBS

Bulbs to plant in autumn

Indispensable for a bulb border are the tulip species, very much longer living than the Dutch hybrids, and with flowers of the utmost brilliance. Many are more suited to the rockery, and for this location *T. dasystemon* and *T. Batalini* are superb little gems. Others are excellent for bedding or for planting in the mixed bulb border. For the back of the border, *T. Eichleri*, of orange-scarlet flowers with a striking black centre, and *T. Hageri*, its copper-coloured flowers shaded with olive green, grow only ten inches high and come into bloom early in April. For planting towards the front of the border, the *T. Kaufmanniana* hybrids are most striking, with their large globes of brilliant hues. The variety 'Elliott' is striking, white petals marked with scarlet; the tiny 'Gaiety', which grows only four inches tall, is of 'Jersey cream' striped with scarlet, the blooms appearing to rest on the soil. A most unusual border variety is *T. praestans* 'Fusilier', its several vivid orange-red blooms appearing together on a nine-inch stem. Three or four bulbs of each variety planted in groups at regular intervals about the border will add splashes of vivid colouring which nothing else can supply.

Groups of the Miniature daffodils, so valuable for growing in small pots and on grassy banks, may also be planted about a border, but the tiniest, such as *Narcissus minimus* and *N. minor*, should be reserved for alpine house and rockery. Several hybrids, for example the fragrant 'Lintie' and 'February Gold', grow rather too tall to come within the scope of this book, but there are many others of great charm, such as *N. cernuus*, a Daffodil known to Stuart gardeners. It bears its nodding flowers of silvery white on nine-inch stems above blue-green foliage. A hybrid well worth growing is 'W. P. Milner', with long cream-coloured trumpet, which grows just under a foot high. For the centre of the border the new 'Hawera', a cross between *N. jonquilla* and *N. triandrus* (the Angel's Tears Daffodil) is delightful, bearing four blooms with unusual reflexed petals to each eight-inch stem. Another gem is 'Beryl', a *N. cyclamineus* hybrid, its globular cups of orange held on eight-inch stems. It should be said that the Miniature daffodils may take two years to become fully established, but are well worth waiting for.

The Grape Hyacinths, always so pleasing when planted with Daffodils, should be set in generous groups. The inexpensive hybrid 'Heavenly Blue', eight inches, has spikes of globular bells of rich gentian blue; 'Cantab' spikes are a pure shade of Cambridge blue. Combining the colourings of both hybrids is the species *Muscari Tubergenianum*, recently introduced from Persia, the top bells of vivid but pale blue, the lower bells, dark blue. As a contrast, plant near them *M. polyanthum album* with white spikes on seven-inch stems.

Also blue is the early flowering Squill, *Scilla sibirica* 'Spring Beauty', twice the height of the alpine squills and bearing its purple-blue spikes in long succession. In bloom with it in early spring is *S. Tubergeniana*, six inches, a new Squill of great beauty and more like a refined Puschkinia. Its porcelain blue bells have petals striped with deep purple. The 'Lebanon Squill', *Puschkinia scilloides*, is sadly neglected yet is one of the most versatile of bulbs, for it is attractive on a rockery, when naturalised in short grass, for pots in the home, and in a border. The flowers, borne on six-inch stems, are white, each petal being striped with clear blue. It remains in bloom for a long season.

The lovely bulbous irises should not be omitted, great favourites for their exquisite colouring. These sturdy little chaps are quite untroubled by the severest of weather. Though *I. Danfordiae* is best planted on a rockery, a group or two planted to the very front of a border will add a splash of brilliant gold during February. And use as liberally as possible the inexpensive violet-scented *I. reticulata*, with blooms on nine-inch stems amid rush-like foliage during March and April. The purple flowers have an orange blotch on the fall petals. A more refined form is the variety, 'Wentworth', but it is rather more expensive.

Snowdrops are welcome almost anywhere in the garden, but whereas the common single and double forms may be liberally used for naturalising, the larger-flowered single species, *Galanthus Elwesii*, its inner segments margined with emerald green, should be planted in the border together with *G. nivalis viridiapice*, the petals this time tipped with green. Another Snowdrop of great beauty is *G. ikariae*, which has broad glossy foliage and globular flowers marked halfway with brilliant green.

Where there is grass for naturalising, the bulb border might be kept for the more select bulbs such as these snowdrops mentioned. Another plant of outstanding charm is *Erythronium tuolumnense*, a species of the Dog's Tooth Violet. It is extremely free flowering and has dark green glossy leaves above which, on twelve-inch stems, cyclamen-like flowers of brilliant golden yellow appear during April.

Equally beautiful is *E. californicum* 'White Beauty', which has rich mottled foliage and large creamy-white flowers with a distinctive chocolate zone at the centre. Two bulbs will cost as much as a packet of twenty cigarettes but will give years of pleasure.

In small pockets about the border plant, as liberally as possible, the Winter Aconite; its golden cups to be found nestling among its emerald green leaves as soon as the first warm rays of sunshine reach the plants in February. The blooms are held on the shortest possible stems, and so may be used to form drifts of brilliant colouring.

There are many more charming little bulbous plants for use in the miniature border. You may add to the original plants as the years pass by until the border will become the most interesting part of the whole garden. For those who garden in the more sheltered districts, south-west of a line drawn from Bristol to Bournemouth, a number of the less hardy bulbs, those described in Chapter 8 may be grown without special protection. Risks may be taken where the border is in a walled garden, possibly facing south. Here, the lovely Tritonia and the brilliantly coloured Sparaxis would be quite happy in well-drained soil if given a thick mulch before winter; these bulbs, natives of the Southern Hemisphere, will be happier with the protection of low shrubs and shrub-like plants such as the dwarf heathers and veronicas. But try to plan for colour throughout the year rather than a profuse display in springtime.

The diagram on p. 61 suggests an arrangement.

2 ft

Lilium Maculatum
Allium Karatav-iense
Crocus Zonatus
Crocus Imperati

Gladiolus Nanus
Narcissus Hawera
Muscari Cantab

Tulipa Eichleri
Tulipa Linifolia
Iris Reticulata

Lilium Maculatum
Colchicum Autumnale Album
Puschkinia Scilloides

Tulipa Praestans Fusilier
Narcissus Beryl
Tulipa Kaufmanniana Brilliant
Crocus Susianus
Galanthus Elwesii

Erythronium Tuolumnense
Tulipa Kauf. Gluck
Narcissus Triandrus

Fritillaria Aphrodite
Narcissus W.P. Milner
Iris Reticulata
Iris Danfordiae

Tulipa Eichleri
Muscari Heavenly Blue

Zephyranthes Candida
Erythronium Californicum White Beauty
Puschkinia Scilloides
Crocus Chrysanthus
T. Kaufmanniana Gaiety

Lilium Maculatum

Fritillaria Pallidiflora
Tulipa Chrysantha
Colchicum Speciosum
Bulbocodium Vernum
Eranthis Guinea Gold

Allium Karataviensis
Scilla Sibirica Spring Beauty

12"   9"   7"   5"   3'

A Border of Miniature Bulbs to Provide Colour throughout the Year

CHAPTER 6

Miniature Bulbs for the Alpine Garden

The value of bulbs in the alpine garden—Making the garden—Planting the bulbs—Suitable bulbs for the alpine garden—Care of the plants—Bulbs for crazy paving

---

The value of bulbs in the alpine garden

It is in the alpine garden that the miniature bulbs are to be seen at their best, for it is here that they find conditions similar to those of their native haunts. There, often high above sea level, they are to be found snuggling up against large boulders for protection from the cold winds of spring. In this country they remain healthy and vigorous and bloom year after year if planted in a well-drained soil; more small bulbs are lost each year through excess moisture remaining about the roots than for any other reason. They grow naturally in pockets of sandy loam overlying rubble, where sufficient moisture will be retained in summer and excess will drain away in winter. In such conditions, the plants will remain healthy almost indefinitely. Dwarf conifer trees may be used to provide a background; the smallest of the alpine bulbs may be used for a trough garden or window box, as described in Chapters 8 and 9.

Plant liberally about the alpine garden for most of the miniatures are admirable in having foliage that is neat and tidy and which dies back without littering the rockery. In a town garden perennial plants are often troubled by deposits of soot, so the fact that the foliage dies down after flowering is a great help. In this respect the compact '*Juliae*' primroses are similar, and for a few weeks in winter they lose their foliage entirely. They should be planted with the bulbs on a town rockery to provide a pleasing carpet for other spring-flowering plants.

The miniature bulbs need less attention than many other alpine plants, such as those of vigorous, trailing habit which tend to over-run their neighbours.

62

MINIATURE BULBS FOR THE ALPINE GARDEN

In gardens not troubled by soot deposits, the evergreen carpeting plants will make admirable ground cover for the bulbs, providing a concealment for the foliage of the bulbs as it dies back, preventing the blooms from being splashed, and keeping down weeds. They will also keep the bulbs cool and moist during periods of sunny weather. A list of carpeting plants is given in Chapter 8, and all may be used in the alpine garden. There are others, not really coarse, which are of rather too vigorous habit for a trough garden. These include the alpine phloxes, particularly *P. Douglasii*, 'May Snow', having sheets of purest white during May and early June. Beneath its foliage should be planted *Muscari armeniacum* 'Cantab'; and with *Phlox Douglasii* 'Violet Queen' plant the pure white *Muscari Argaei album*, which flowers well into June.

The early flowering Kabschia or Cushion saxifrages are excellent for planting with miniature bulbs, forming hummocks of silvery green and blooming from March until mid-May. With *Saxifraga Jenkinsae*, having blooms of clear pink, try the tiny Dalmatian Hyacinth, as the azure blue spikes flower at the same time; or plant *Iris reticulata* and *Iris histrioides* (both purple) among the *Burseriana* saxifrages, with white and yellow flowers.

The dainty Dresden China daisy, with its buttons of palest pink, looks quite enchanting alongside *Crocus chrysanthus* 'Blue Pearl'. For later in the year, *Nierembergia rivularis*, which forms mats of dark green on which sit stemless white cups during early autumn, acts as a pleasing foil to the lavender flowers of *Crocus cancellatus* and *C. nudiflorus*, whose blooms appear before the leaves.

Another good combination is of the little perennial candytuft, *Iberis Jordani*, having a mat of white flowers during May, with the Persian tulip, having several orange and yellow blooms to each four-inch stem. Another lovely alpine garden tulip is *T. pulchella*, four inches, with star-like flowers of pinky-lilac during March. Plant it in a pocket of leaf mould and sand with the tiny *Primula Clarkei* which has almost stemless flowers of glowing pink also in March.

For May and June flowering, another delightful combination is *Fritillaria citrina*, with bright lemon-yellow flowers, and *Viola gracilis major*, with purple, violet-like blooms. In flower at the same time is the prostrate *Veronica rupestris*, 'Mauve Queen'. There is also a pink-flowered form, 'Mrs. Holt'. For *F. citrina*, see page 39.

A colourful combination in a dry, sunny situation includes *Anomatheca cruenta* with the creeping, aromatic thymes; *T. serpyllum*

63

coccineus with masses of brilliant crimson blooms, 'Snowdrift' with white flowers, all flowering together.

There are miniature bulbs to bloom throughout the year, but bulbs of rampant habit, which multiply rapidly by seeding or through the formation of bulblets, are best confined to the shrubbery, or planted beneath trees where their rapid increase will be welcome. There are so many other lovely bulbous plants for the alpine garden that the *Corydalis* and Bluebell and most of the Anemone species should be omitted, in favour of less hardy bulbs; these would not require lifting and storing over winter if planted among rockery stones and with shrubby alpine plants (as described earlier) for protection.

Instead of carpeting plants, limestone chippings placed around and over the bulbs during winter will provide protection for the less hardy bulbs, suppress annual weeds, and prevent soil from being splashed on to the petals and foliage.

Where miniature bulbs and such accommodating plants as the Saxifrages and Sempervivums and other shade-lovers are to be used, a colourful rockery can be made in partial shade, possibly against the wall of an outbuilding, or close to tall trees—though not too close, since drip from trees may cause waterlogging.

An alpine garden may also be made at the end of a garden, or to divide one part of the garden from another. Here, raised above ground level, the plants are seen to great advantage. A small, neat garden may be made on either side of stone steps, or as an alternative to a low grassy bank; or any ground having a pronounced slope may be made interesting by the use of suitable stone and miniature bulbs.

One of the best-devised small alpine gardens I have seen was made on either side of a flight of stone steps leading down to a dell. The not-quite-overhanging branches of mature trees provided a grotto-like appearance, and throughout the year this garden was full of the rich colour of shade-loving plants, brilliant with the blossoms of Hardy cyclamen, Dog's Tooth Violets, the Chionodoxas and Dwarf hyacinths. Snowdrops and Winter aconites carpeted the ground in their season. As the trees came into leaf the filtered sunlight shone down on the brilliant blue of the scillas and the bright yellow of the daffodils to produce a most striking effect with the pale green foliage of the beech trees. Of course the planting was lavish.

16. The dainty pale lemon blooms of *Fritillaria citrina* are borne on five-inch stems. A good pot plant. Flowering in April

17. *Tulipa tarda* (*dasystemon*). A very beautiful Dwarf Tulip producing a cluster of up to four blooms from each bulb. The petals relax in the warmth of the sun, so that the flowers resemble white stars with centres of vivid golden yellow. Flowers in April

18. *Tulipa biflora*. Each stem bears two to four starry white blooms at a height of only six inches

19. *Erythronium dens-canis*. 'Dog's Tooth Violet'

Making an alpine garden

An alpine garden must look as though it were a part of the mountains where the plants naturally grow, not a jumble of rock from a landslide, where nothing will flourish. One made on a flat site to hold bulbs should look like the bed of a stream, or a level outcrop where the rock has weathered into hollows in which the fine fragments have gathered, and plants have begun to build up humus and so are able to flourish between the harder portions that have resisted wind and weather.

So whatever the rock is, it must look as though it were an outcrop from a solid mass below the soil, even though it comes to you in many small fragments. Limestone and sandstone are laid down in layers by water, and these layers should slope in the same directions so the best effect is secured by creating a slope which all the fragments follow, of course not too geometrically.

Westmorland limestone is excellent, for its 'layers' show clearly; it has many crevices to take plants such as Sedums and Sempervivums; it resists frost; and its grey colour contrasts beautifully with small and brilliant corollas. Sandstone is quite good too, and often cheaper, but it looks red and raw for a long while, and frost gets into it and flakes off great chunks. Granite always looks like a graveyard, and flint is worst of all. Garden contractors usually stock Westmorland or Cheddar stone, both good. Westmorland limestone may be obtained from alpine garden contractors who will generally have small quantities for disposal and will deliver it.

Where making a small alpine garden, it is better to use stones of average size and as near as possible of the same size throughout. Avoid the use of dozens of small pieces, as it is not easy to arrange these in a natural-looking 'outcrop'. A quantity of fresh loamy soil, preferably sterilized, will probably be obtainable from a local nurseryman and with this should be incorporated some grit to encourage drainage and a small proportion of moist peat to help to retain summer moisture. A quantity of boiler ash or similar material should be available for drainage at the base of the rockery, and this may be collected and stored until required.

Once the stone is on the site, the making of the alpine garden should proceed slowly. It is generally believed that the more haphazard the stone is set, the better will be the effect. This is far from being the case, for so many things need to be considered beyond mere casualness of disposal.

E   65

A rock garden on the flat should face south if possible, but if this is away from the view of the house it can face in any direction. Dig out the soil four inches deep, keeping the upper layer to make bought loam and peat go further, and taking great care to get out all perennial weed roots, especially those of couch-grass and convolvulus.

Even if it can come up only a little towards the back the appearance is still improved because the plants and rock at the back are displayed better. So making a dry wall a foot high, even behind a garden twelve feet long, and building a slope towards it with the removed soil, helps considerably.

Fill the excavation half full with a two-inch layer all over of small clinker, boiler ash, or domestic ashes sifted to remove the dust, for you do not want a solid path, but a means of drainage. Then consider your rock, which for a flat site should be in long flat pieces—a rock bank or a steep rock garden wants them with tall 'faces', a flat garden less face and more top.

The 'face' of limestone is the surface showing the layers, with those that are softer eroded away by the rain driving against the front of the rock. The 'top' is where the rain beats down on it, or where standing water wore it away, and this will have rounded holes in it and good crevices for planting, while the underside will be jagged or flat where it was broken off the solid rock.

A good rock garden stone may be 'two-faced' where a side was exposed to weather, but always a face should look to the front, and the tops upward. This applies to all rock, but because the layers or 'strata' of limestone show so clearly, rock gardens where this elementary principle has been disregarded are an offence to the eye.

You can build a flat site downwards, upwards or sideways, bedding the rocks into the drainage layer so that they look like the hard parts sticking up, with the soil in between where the bulbs will grow as the depressions into which the rock fragments have been washed.

Have each rock higher at the face than at the back, so that it has a slant away from the way of the slope. This is because when rock slopes the other way it would not show faces, and it would trap no soil in pockets—the water would sweep everything clear. Only a little difference in height is enough, but it should be roughly the same for every stone.

Instead of dotting your rocks about, concentrate them, so that they fit together one behind the other as the sides of a ravine. Have a few across the mouth of the ravine, faces forward, with a flat planting space behind them as if there were a waterfall over the two-inch-high cliff. Use the long rocks pointing the way the 'stream' flowed, but always face forward with the top upwards.

Because the site is flat the strata lines on the faces need to be flat, but if you have a slope two ways, you can follow this, with the strata lines parallel with the slopes. Always think of your rock garden as one big rock with parts of it showing through the soil, and then it will be fun to build—a kind of landscape painting in grey stone.

Then put on the soil, three or four inches deep, ramming it firmly round the rocks; for they need to be firm enough not to move when you tread on them for weeding. In the spaces between plant your bulbs, and if there are any rocks with good tall faces have them fairly high on your slope, and plant low growing bulbs in front of them, so that yellow or bright blue flowers show against the grey stone.

To make an alpine garden on a low bank, insert the stone into the bank after removing the grass. You should aim at giving the completed rockery as natural an appearance as possible by following the suggestions already made. Here, the stones should again be placed with their flat surface uppermost and each should slope gently in the same direction. It may not, however, be possible to build up the stones as gradually as desired (for the more gradual the slope, the more natural the appearance) since the slope must be determined by the fall of the ground. It may be possible to make an extension by adding soil at the base, thus lessening the acuteness of the angle where the bank is unduly steep. If the grass carries on where the alpine garden terminates, an alpine lawn might be made, to be planted with early flowering bulbs which will permit the grass to be cut at suitable seasons.

An alpine garden at the foot of a wall or in a corner should be built up by degrees, and it will first be necessary to provide a foundation. The core of the garden may be of material which will have little value for use elsewhere and indeed most new gardens contain quantities of stone, broken bricks and mortar and all manner of unwanted material left behind by the builder. An old property, too, generally abounds in broken pots and glass and other refuse which will need to be removed and which, with boiler ash and clinker, will be ideal for making a base for an alpine garden. Where no rubbish is available, a load of broken brick from a building site will be necessary. This will make for efficient drainage and help to raise the garden. Over this fresh loam is tipped, then the stones are placed as previously described. Do not attempt to make the garden too high, and do not use too much stone or pieces that are too large; for what would well be a most pleasing improvement to a colourless part of the garden, would thus become an uninteresting mass of stone.

Planting the bulbs

The planting may begin with dwarf conifers which will grow little more than twelve to eighteen inches tall. A most beautiful tree is the dwarf Norway Spruce, *Picea excelsa nana compacta*, its horizontal branches giving it a delightfully rounded appearance. *P. Veitchii* forms a dainty rounded tree and has olive green foliage. The dwarf evergreen Yew, *Thuya laetivirens*, is extremely handsome too, its foliage having a moss-like appearance. There are others, all of which make a delightful foil for the bulbs and plants.

Then plant the bulbs in the pockets formed by the stones, setting them in groups of four or five for those bulbs forming upright grass-like leaves, and in groups of two or three where the plants are of low, bushy habit, e.g. *Erythronium dens-canis*. Plant in June and July those bulbs which come into bloom in autumn and early winter; plant in autumn, which is the most suitable time for making up the alpine garden, those that bloom in spring. Observe the correct planting depths, though where the alpine garden affords a certain amount of protection and the soil is well drained, greater liberties may be taken in this respect.

Suitable bulbs for the alpine garden

Among the most charming bulbs for the alpine garden, where they may be given that little extra attention they would not otherwise receive, are the smallest of the Miniature daffodils. They are best taken up and planted soon after they have flowered, like Snowdrops, being divided while in full leaf and replanted with the minimum of delay.

Narcissus minimus, which grows less than three inches tall, is a little plant of charming delicacy. It is the first of the Miniature daffodils to bloom, bearing its tiny golden trumpets before the end of February. Parkinson tells us that the first bulbs were brought to this country at the beginning of the seventeenth century by a Frenchman, Francis le Veau, 'the honestest root gatherer that ever came over to us' as he is so charmingly described by Parkinson. *N. juncifolius*, the miniature rush-leaf daffodil from the Pyrenees, with flattish little blooms on four-inch stems is also at home in the alpine garden. The flowers are deliciously fragrant as are those of *N. canaliculatus*, a charming Polyanthus narcissus which has four blooms to each stem, their white perianths enhanced by a tiny golden cup. Is there any plant more fairy-like? *N. minor* is also right for the alpine garden. It is very early to bloom; its twisted perianth and lobed trumpet are of deepest yellow. The 'Hoop Petticoat' Daffodils are also most elegant. They bear their flowers on six-inch stems, the first to bloom being *N. bulbocodium romieuxii*. Then follows the lemon-yellow form, *citrinus* and later, *conspicuus*, having conical trumpets of brilliant gold. Natives of Southern France and Spain, these lovely Miniature daffodils require a well-drained sandy soil containing some peat. There are many others, and early to bloom is *N. lobularis*, which has a sulphur perianth and yellow trumpet, likewise the new hybrid 'Wee Bee', with its yellow self-coloured flowers. A rare and extremely beautiful species from Morocco, *N. Watieri*, has a tiny pure white flower of 'crystalline texture' and is a gem for the rock garden or for pans in the alpine house. It is late to bloom. The lovely *N. rupicola*, which will seed itself when established, should also be planted. It has bright yellow flowers with six-lobed corona on four-inch stems. The Cyclamen-flowered narcissus, *N. cyclamineus*, with its reflexed perianth, should also be included though it is happiest in a damp situation near a pond or stream.

The Chionodoxas should be planted close to the Daffodils for they will be in bloom at the same time, the brilliant blue colouring of their flowers providing an attractive contrast to the golden yellow. Their native haunt is Greece. It is a most valuable little flower in that it is quite unresentful of the cold winds and sleet showers of early spring, and unlike the crocus it refuses to close up its flowers to protect itself from the elements. Its delicate-looking blooms completely deceive with their appearance, for they are among the toughest of all flowers and can be seen from afar. The rockery well suits the 'Glory of the Snow', for it enjoys a more open, sunny situation than most of the miniature flowering bulbs, and it likes a well-drained soil. The blooms are of such distinctive, and rather harsh, colouring that they should be kept quite separate. Unlike the Crocuses, the blooms are rarely troubled by birds nor do the bulbs prove an attraction for mice. They have, in fact, 'no vices'.

First into bloom, early in March, is *C. sardensis*, choice flowers with their glistening white centre of rich Gentian blue. Then follows, at the month's end, *C. luciliae*, the vivid blue flowers with their striking white eye borne in dainty sprays at a height of four inches. There is also an attractive pale pink form, *rosea*. *C. gigantea* is at its best throughout April. It is taller growing than the others, with soft lavender-blue flowers on six-inch stems; it seeds itself abundantly and is best planted in the shrubbery.

The miniatures of the crocus species are ideal plants for the alpine garden and they may be seen in bloom from September, when *C. zonatus* comes into flower, until the following May, finishing with the sapphire-blue *C. Tomasinianus*. For October flowering the lovely *C. pulchellus*, with its lavender flowers and white anthers, and *C. medius*, with its rich violet blooms and orange stigmas, should be included in every rockery. For November, the sweetly scented *C. longiflorus* should be planted. Then follows the sweetly-scented *C. imperati*, its outer petals fawn coloured, feathered with violet. The dainty *C. ancyrensis* is always at its loveliest where given the protection of stone. It comes into bloom with the first warm February sunshine, its tiny tubes of burnt-orange providing a most welcome appearance at this time of the year, and it remains long in bloom. Flowering at the same time is *C. Fleischeri*, a particular favourite of all who know it. Its starry white flowers have brilliant scarlet stigmas and it remains long in bloom.

C. biflorus, native of the Mediterranean shores, its silvery-lilac petals earning for it the name of 'Cloth of Silver' crocus, is also just right for the rockery. It was well known to Parkinson. One of the last to bloom and ideal for a rockery with its small, neat flowers of brilliant golden yellow, is *C. Olivieri* 'Jamie', a variety of recent introduction and extremely free-flowering.

For early spring flowering, the tiny *Iris Danfordiae* must surely find a place on every rockery. It was named after a Mrs. Danford who discovered it growing in the Taurus Mountains in the 1880's when it immediately received an Award of Merit from the Royal Horticultural Society. The reason why it has never attained the popularity of *I. reticulata* is that the bulbs flower for only one year, and it may be two years before the newly formed bulblets come into bloom again. For all that, it is well worth waiting for the rich yellow flowers borne on three-inch stems. To prevent splashing of the bloom, the compost should be covered with chippings before the flower buds appear in the early New Year, unless carpeting plants have been used. Its bulbs are 'netted' like those of *I. reticulata*, and they should be planted into pockets of lime rubble to get the best results.

Iris reticulata is a most handsome early spring bulb for the rockery, for planting in short grass, or growing in pots in the home or alpine house, where its delicious violet fragrance is appreciated as much as its beautifully coloured bloom. It bears its blooms, like those of the Dutch irises in miniature, on eight-inch stems; its rush-like foliage is neat and upright so that half a dozen bulbs may be planted in an area no larger than a saucer to give a display of great beauty during March. With the royal purple, 'Wentworth', plant the glorious pale blue 'Cantab'.

With *I. Danfordiae* plant *I. histrioides major* which flowers at the same time. Its bloom is similar in colour and form to that of *I. reticulata* but is almost twice the size, on a six-inch stem.

Also in bloom early in spring is *Scilla Tubergeniana*, its pale blue flowers on four-inch stems having a dark blue stripe down the petals. The dainty *Scilla bifolia* should also be planted on the rockery, its darkest blue flowers acting as a foil for the pink flowered *rosea*. In bloom at the same time will be *S. sibirica*, its brilliant blue flowers on three-inch stems. Plant with it the pure white form, *alba*.

For April and May flowering, the miniature hyacinths are most attractive. *H. amethystinus* is the true Alpine Hyacinth from the Pyrenees, of which Reginald Farrer, the great authority on alpine plants, wrote, 'without rivalry or comparison, stands bright amongst the loveliest bulbs we have. . . .' Indeed it does, its clear azure-blue bells being borne in profusion on seven-inch stems. There is also a white form, *alba*, and *H. azureus*, a month earlier, with little spikes of Cambridge blue. H. *dalmaticus* blooms in March even in the most exposed garden. It has thick spikes of azure-blue on six-inch stems, and is quite unlike most miniature hyacinths and the closely related Grape Hyacinths. Of these *Muscari polyanthum album* is particularly charming with spikes of pure white on six-inch stems during the later days of April, a useful contrast for the hybrid, 'Heavenly Blue'.

Winter Aconites may be planted freely and no alpine garden would be complete without at least one pocket planted with the Hardy cyclamen and the Dog's Tooth Violet.

For a splash of brilliant colour in the alpine garden, the Tulip species stands supreme and it is difficult to understand just why they are not more widely planted for this purpose. These little plants are

71

just right for planting in groups of three or four with the grey tufa stone for a background. *T. pulchella* from Persia, the home of the Tulip, is the first to bloom, and with *T. persica* is one of the smallest. It is in bloom by mid-March, its urn-shaped blooms of pale mauve on four-inch stems opening flat in the sun to reveal a bright yellow centre. Then follows *T. biflora* from the Caucasus, each six-inch stem having three starry white flowers which remain in bloom over a long period. Then in early April comes *T. Batalini*, expensive but charming. Its creamy yellow blooms are on six-inch stems above unique grey foliage. With it plant *T. chrysantha* from the Himalayas; it has dainty yellow blooms shaded cherry-red on the outside. If possible, try to include the most unusual *T. dasystemon*, with several pale yellow flowers shaded with grey and green on the exterior on each six-inch stem. This is one of the most beautiful of all alpine garden plants.

To plant with the yellow- and white-flowering Tulips, but where its shining scarlet blooms (on six-inch stems) will not clash with other flowers, *T. Maximowiczii* is extremely gay, so is *T. linifolia*, with glowing crimson flowers early in May.

Latest of all is the Persian Tulip, *T. persica*, of which Parkinson wrote in his *Paradisus*: 'This rare tulip wherewith we have been but lately acquainted'. In partial shade it will still be in bloom on June 1st. It is a little gem for the rockery and for edging a small path, with several blooms to each four-inch stem. The flowers are vivid golden-yellow, shaded with bronze on the outside, and are deliciously fragrant. Bulbs will cost 2s. 6d. each but do plant at least one group about the rockery, for there is no more rewarding plant.

For early summer, *Brodiaea grandiflora* offers its umbels of deep blue during June when the garden will be devoid of the brilliant colouring of the spring months, though there will be many summer flowering alpine plants in bloom. Plant with it the equally pleasing *B. crocea*, with umbels of lemon-yellow flowers on six-inch stems during May and June. Though a native of California, it is perfectly hardy.

The smallest of the Flowering Garlics, *Allium ostrowskianum*, is a most attractive plant for a rockery, and, like the Brodiaeas, bears its heads of deep rosy-red on six-inch stems during June. More difficult to obtain, but well worth trying to find, is *A. cyaneum*, a native of China. It has bright green leaves, and the flowers of vivid blue have an attractive green eye.

MINIATURE BULBS FOR THE ALPINE GARDEN

To bridge the gap between the early summer and the first of the autumn-flowering bulbs, plant *Cyclamen europaeum* for bloom during July and August, and several groups of that dainty South African bulbous plants, *Anomatheca cruenta*, which during the same period bears bright salmon-red flowers, blotched with crimson.

Care of the plants and bulbs

Having made the first planting of bulbs in October, it will be advisable to wait until they are making growth in spring before the autumn-flowering bulbs are planted and the alpine plants set out. The end of March and throughout April is the most suitable time to plant alpines, for they will then grow away to a good start and form a vigorous rooting system with no trouble from hard frost.

If the bulbs have been planted in circles or in triangular form, spacing them about three inches apart, there will be room at the centre for a carpeting or some other alpine plant. This will usually be pot-grown and may be planted with the soil ball intact. This should be inserted well into the soil and made quite firm.

Do not forget to name the plant and the bulbs by means of small wooden labels on which the plant name is written in indelible ink. Also, if the compost appears dry, water in the alpine plants and ensure that they do not lack moisture until they are thoroughly established. In fact, both the bulbs and the plants will appreciate an occasional spraying during dry weather.

To maintain both bulbs and plants in a healthy condition, they should be provided with a mulch of peat or leaf mould to which is added a small amount of decayed cow manure or used hops. This is worked into the soil around the plants and over the bulbs, where they are not covered with carpeting plants. The foliage of the bulbs may be partially hidden by pressing it beneath nearby plants or by pinning it to the soil as it dies back. It may also be hidden, as described earlier, by using plants of shrubby habit which grow about six inches tall. If the spring and early summer-flowering plants are planted in the same group as those that bloom in later summer and early autumn, this will help to hide the dying foliage of the early-flowering bulbs, which must not be entirely removed until it has had time to die right back.

Cloches may also be used to bring various plants, including bulbs, into bloom before their natural time; but remember that you are dealing with alpine plants, used to cold regions, and at all times ample supplies of air must be admitted. The use of an open-ended cloche will help to bring the bulbs into bloom a little earlier than normally and protect the more tender winter flowering plants from fog and soot deposits. Cloches are also useful for giving any newly planted alpines some protection from cold, drying spring wings until they become established. More plants are harmed by drying winds in spring when producing the new season's growth than by any other cause. If no glass is available, even twigs and small branches of evergreens inserted into the soil around the plants will provide much-appreciated protection.

It is advisable to remove from the rockery all leaves which may have fallen from nearby trees in late autumn and which become lodged about the stones and plants. They not only look untidy but will become saturated, and may cause nearby plants and bulbs to decay should the winter be unduly wet.

Provided both plants and bulbs are given the care necessary for their continued health, they should remain vigorous and free flowering for many years without the need to lift and divide. Overcrowding should, however, be guarded against and where this occurs, the bulbs may be thinned by lifting a number from each clump so as to allow more room for those left in the ground. Those which have been lifted may be divided and replanted elsewhere.

Bulbs for crazy paving

Where space is limited, bulbs may be used in pockets of soil about a path of crazy paving stone, two or three bulbs of the smallest species and varieties being planted in each pocket.

When laying a path of crazy paving, begin by marking out the necessary length and width, then remove several inches of soil, depending on (a) the depth of stone, and (b) whether it is proposed to lay the stone on to a thin bed of concrete.

The question of the concrete bed is all-important, for not only will it provide a firmer foundation which will prevent various stones from falling below the original level, which in time they so frequently do, but it will prevent the appearance of grass and weeds which are the curse of crazy paving. No matter how well the stone is laid, placing each stone tightly to its neighbours with only the minimum of soil exposed, weeds will eventually push their way up from between the stones and will be almost impossible to clear. And there is no more irksome task in the garden than trying to clear a well-laid crazy paving path of grass and weeds. The concreting will add slightly to the cost in the first instance and will mean more labour, but will be more than worth while. Pockets between the stones may be left free of concrete at irregular intervals to take the bulbs, but do not overdo this; a few look much better than too many. The still wet concrete can be removed from the pockets after sections of the path are laid.

First select your stones before the work is to begin and if possible place them into something like order by the side of the path. Small stones may be placed into convenient heaps to be used to fill in any gaps. A better job can be made of a terrace where either flags or crazy paving stone is being used if first a solid foundation of clinker or crushed brick or stone is made. This means taking out an extra two or three inches of soil, but a clinker foundation will make a much better base over which to place the concrete. Even where no concrete is being used, a clinker base will prove of untold value in providing additional drainage, especially if the path is at all low lying. The soil may be used to fill up the pockets, but a prepared compost would be better.

Apart from a good spade, the only tool needed will be the important spirit level which will ensure a neater and more professional job, with stones laid level. Obtain a builder's 'level' large enough to span across the path so that the top of the stone may be kept level with the sides of the bed. From the beginning of operations, make use of the level, right from the time the clinker base is put down, for this will ensure that the concrete will also be level and will make the final laying of the stone a much easier matter. Be sure to have the flattest surface of the stone to the top, and of course the sides should be kept as near straight as possible. A neat job can be made by laying (in cement) a row of bricks down each side of the path, placing them on their sides. The contrast in colour of brick and stone adds to the finished effect and will help to prevent the soil from falling on to the concrete while this is being placed into position; it also makes the laying of the level stone much easier. Remember to set the stones as close to each other as possible, for if too much concrete is used to point the path on completion, it will spoil the effect. If the stone can be laid close, no pointing needs to be done beyond the filling-up of those pockets into which you have no intention of setting a plant. My own method is to do the planting as the work proceeds. First make a satisfactory base which is quite level, then lay the stone in possibly six-foot lengths, completely finishing the stretch in every way before continuing with the next six feet or so. Pockets for bulbs should have the concrete removed while still wet and the aperture should be filled up with compost.

The compost mixture should be of leaf mould, soil, decayed manure and sand in equal parts and should be placed between the stones to a depth of at least four inches, otherwise there will not be a sufficient root run for the bulbs. Before the compost is added, a few pieces of crushed brick or mortar should be put in to encourage drainage. Firm the compost. Two or three bulbs should be planted in each pocket, the most suitable being the Winter Aconites, Snowdrops, the smallest of the crocus miniatures, *Bulbocodium vernum*, *Muscari argaei album*, *Hyacinthus dalmaticus*, *Oxalis adenophylla* and *Scilla verna*. If several of the carpeting plants are also used, and the Sedums and Thymes are outstanding in this respect, the crazy paving will be colourful for long periods. These bulbs and the following will be equally suitable for the alpine garden. All are of dwarf, dainty habit and have neat, tidy foliage:

Name	Flowering Time	Height
Allium cyaneum	July–August	4 ins.
Anomatheca cruenta	July–August	5–6 ins.
Brodiaea crocea	May–June	5–6 ins.
„ minor	June	5–6 ins.
Bulbocodium vernum	March	3 ins.
Chionodoxa luciliae	March–April	4 ins.
„ sardensis	March	4 ins.
„ tmoli	April	4 ins.
Crocus ancyrensis	Feb.–March	2 ins.
„ Balansae	March	1½ ins.
„ Fleischeri	Feb.–April	2 ins.
„ Korolkowi	Jan.–March	1½ ins.
„ laevigatus	Dec.–Feb.	3 ins.
„ medius	October	3 ins.
„ minimus	March–April	1½ ins.
„ nudiflorus	Oct.–Nov.	3 ins.
„ ochroleucus	Nov.–Dec.	2 ins.
„ olivieri	April–May	2 ins.
„ sativus	October	2 ins.

MINIATURE BULBS FOR THE ALPINE GARDEN

Name	Flowering Time	Height
Crocus vernus	March	2 ins.
Cyclamen alpinum	Dec.–Feb.	3 ins.
„ *Atkinsii*	Dec.–March	3–4 ins.
„ *cilicium*	Sept.–Nov.	3 ins.
„ *graecum*	July–Sept.	4 ins.
Eranthus cilicica	Feb.–March	2 ins.
„ *hyemalis*	Jan.–Feb.	2 ins.
Erythronium dens-canis	March–April	6 ins.
„ *Hendersonii*	April	4 ins.
Fritillaria citrina	April–May	5–6 ins.
„ *pudica*	April–May	4 ins.
Galanthus Allenii	April	3–4 ins.
„ *byzantinus*	Dec.–Jan.	4 ins.
„ *latifolius*	March–April	3 ins.
„ *nivalis*	Feb.–March	5 ins.
Hyacinthus azureus	April	5 ins.
„ *dalmaticus*	April	4 ins.
Iris Bakeriana	Jan.–Feb.	6 ins.
„ *Danfordiae*	February	4 ins.
„ *histrioides*	March	6 ins.
„ *reticulata*	March–April	6 ins.
Muscari argaei album	May–June	4 ins.
„ *armeniacum*	April–May	6 ins.
„ *polyanthus album*	April–May	5–6 ins.
Narcissus bulbocodium	March–April	6 ins.
„ *canaliculatus*	April	6 ins.
„ *capax plenus*	April	6 ins.
„ *juncifolius*	April	4 ins.
„ *minimus*	Feb.–March	4 ins.
„ *nanus*	March–April	6 ins.
„ *rupicola*	April	4 ins.
„ *triandrus*	April–May	6 ins.
„ *Watieri*	May	4 ins.
Puschkinia scilloides	March–May	4 ins.
Scilla bifolia	Feb.–March	6 ins.
„ *Tubergeniana*	Feb.–March	5 ins.
„ *verna*	April	4 ins.
Tulipa australis	April	6 ins.
„ *Batalini*	April	4 ins.

MINIATURE BULBS FOR THE ALPINE GARDEN

Name	Flowering Time	Height
Tulipa biflora	March–April	5 ins.
„ *dasystemon*	April–May	6 ins.
„ *linifolia*	May	6 ins.
„ *Maximowiczii*	April	6 ins.
„ *persica*	May	3 ins.
„ *pulchella*	March–April	4 ins.
„ *Wilsoniana*	May	6 ins.

CHAPTER 7

Bedding Schemes with Dwarf Bulbs

The use of bulbs for bedding—Ideas for spring colour—Summer bedding schemes—Anemones for bedding—The ranunculus—'Multiflora' begonias

The use of bulbs for bedding

For the small garden in particular, the miniature bulbs may be freely planted in small beds in exactly the same way as for the larger Tulips and Hyacinths. True, many of the bulbous flowering miniatures will be suitable only for naturalising, as their loose, informal habit disqualifies them as bedding plants, while there are bulbs which will take fully a year to become established in their new quarters before blooming. In this category may be included the Hardy cyclamen and the Miniature daffodils with but one or two exceptions, and thus they would be unsuitable for bedding. There are also those bulbous plants which prefer the shaded, sheltered woodlands to the more open situation of town garden flower beds, which generally have to contend with full sunshine for most of the day. Whichever plants are used they will have to contend, in most instances, with the poor, dry conditions of a town garden, though much may be done to enrich the soil and improve moisture conservation with supplies of humus in the form of peat, decayed manure, used hops or material from the garden compost heap.

For the garden to be as labour saving and the beds as colourful as possible, inter-planting should be done. In this way spring flowering bulbs may be grown with other spring-flowering plants, together with such plants and bulbs as will continue the display until the end of summer and possibly well into autumn. The bulbs will require lifting and replacing only when they tend to have exhausted the soil. This may not be for several years if the bulbs have been planted in ground which has been well prepared and is well drained.

The most economical associates for the bulbs will be perennials which may be left down for several years with the bulbs. As most of

79

the miniatures will vary between six and ten inches in height, and will be in bloom during the spring and early weeks of summer, height and flowering time of associated plants must be taken into account. The height of plants which will continue the display when the spring-flowering bulbs have finished is of no importance, for by then the bulbs will begin to die back and their unsightly foliage will be hidden by these summer-flowering plants.

Ideas for spring colour

Among the most useful of all flowering plants to use with bulbs will be the Pansies and Violas. Violas will prove longer lasting and remain longer in bloom. To plant with the winter-flowering bulbs such as *Crocus ochroleucus* or *C. imperati*, choose pansies or violas classed as winter-flowering, and which begin to bloom from an early-summer sowing as the sun begins to lose its warmth in November. The yellow- and white-flowered varieties will bloom freely during mid-winter and they look most attractive planted with lavender- and blue-flowered Crocuses. They also make a good carpeter for a bed of purple *Iris reticulata*, March-blooming. Plant the violas six inches apart with the bulbs between them, either directly into the open ground or into small pots inserted into the bed with the rim of the pots just below soil level. In this way, if one does not mind the additional work, the pots may be lifted, after flowering, and replaced with later-flowering bulbs (or with summer bedding plants) so as to prolong the bedding display.

Most spring-flowering bulbs carry little foliage, so the Violas will be useful as a ground cover, being fully evergreen. The plants will help to hide the bare soil during winter and will also prevent splash-ing. Another stand-by plant in bloom from the early New Year, in the most exposed gardens, is the Polyanthus-primrose 'Barrowby Gem', with trusses of pale yellow blooms tinged with green on six-inch stems. Plant it with *Iris reticulata* and the fragrance of their flowers will combine to permeate a small garden on a calm spring day, especially after rain.

A most beautiful display may be obtained from planting the richly coloured Tulip species with dwarf *Juliae* primroses which, like the winter-flowering violas, will form a carpet of bright green during springtime. For a striking effect, plant the large-flowered *T. Kauf-manniana* 'Scarlet Elegance', with vermilion-scarlet flowers on eight-

20. *Narcissus minimus.* The smallest of all narcissi. A perfect miniature daffodil two–three inches high

21. *Puschkinia libanotica*. The 'Lebanon' or 'Striped' Squill. The hyacinth-like spikes consist of a dozen or more flowers having a deep silver-white petal. Flowers in April

22. *Narcissus triandrus albus.* The 'Angels' Tears' Daffodil

23. *Narcissus bulbocodium conspicuus.* The 'Yellow Hoop-petticoat' Daffodil. A quaint flower of rich yellow held on six-inch stems. Rush-like foliage. A good pot plant. Flowers March–April

inch stems (March and April) together with the *Juliae* primrose 'Snow Cushion', its bright green foliage studded with white blooms, also March and April; or with the golden-yellow *T. Kaufmanniana aurea*, plant the new *Juliae* primrose 'Murray's Blue Riband', which has masses of bright mid-blue flowers with a crimson ring around the eye. Another scheme combines a compact primrose, 'E. R. Janes', deep salmon-pink, with *T. Kaufmanniana* 'Shakespeare', of almost exactly the same hue. These lovely Tulips bloom on only six- to eight-inch stems and, like the Primroses, remain long in bloom.

To bloom in April, the brilliant *Fosteriana* Tulips are outstanding, though the smallest is 'Princeps', with scarlet flower, of golden centre. It grows only nine inches tall; the foliage is shining dark green. Plant with this tulip the white form of the dainty Double Daisies of which 'Rob Roy' (red) and 'Dresden China' (pink) are the best known; or raise from seed the new Double Daisy, 'Pomponette', its flowers, like those of 'Rob Roy', tight buttons which are a great improvement on those large, untidy, shaggy blooms of the older type Double Daisy. The Polyanthus should not be forgotten, for the modern strains continue to bloom well into June. In this respect, the American 'Barnhaven' strains are outstanding, the blooms having a diversity and clearness of colouring not to be found in any other strain. For a spectacular display plant the American 'Wine Red' Polyanthus, the large blooms of a deep shade of port wine, with the *T. Kaufmanniana* hybrid 'Johann Strauss', which has large creamy white flowers. In soil which suits them well, these lovely Tulips will not require lifting and replanting each year but may be left to come up season after season.

The miniature Hyacinths make charming plants for bedding display during the latter days of March and on through June, to provide continuity of flowering between the spring flowering bulbs and the first appearance of the summer bedding plants. Outstanding among these lovely plants is *H. amethystinus*, with spikes of amethyst-blue on eight-inch stems. It is most attractive planted among a bed of yellow-flowering Violas and should be planted with those bulbs which bloom earlier in the year.

Summer bedding schemes

Those who have retired to spend their days among their plants will not be put off by the additional work occasioned where later-flowering bulbs, grown in pots, are used to replace those which bloom earlier and which may also be grown in pots. One such plant, which will provide rich colour throughout June and into July, is the *Tritonia crocata* from South Africa. There is a danger that the bulbs may decay during a long wet period in winter and so they are best brought on in 60-size pots, planting four to each pot, and these should be placed in an improvised frame. Or the pots may be kept in a shed over winter, keeping the compost only just moist. The bulbs may be planted in the beds in their pots; they begin to show their flower buds in May. 'Prince of Orange' is the outstanding variety and has branching racemes of glowing scarlet on ten-inch stems.

Plant the *Brodiaeas* with *Tritonia crocata*, the deep blue flowered *B. grandiflora* and *B. laxa*, with umbels of purple-blue flowers on ten-inch stems throughout June. In a favourably situated garden, the *Tritonia* may be planted directly into open ground beds where the soil is light and well drained. *Lilium maculatum* might take over when these plants have finished flowering, say several bulbs of the crimson-flowered 'Mahogany' and the orange *bicolor*, four bulbs of each being sufficient to give rich colour to a small raised bed.

The use of summer-flowering perennials with the bulbs will not only contribute to the display but they will play their part in making the garden as labour saving as possible. They should be used together with those which bloom in spring. Thus they will take over where the spring-flowering plants leave off and will also help to suppress annual weeds.

A useful plant of perennial habit is *Campanula lactiflora*, 'Pouffe', which will remain in bloom from mid-June until September. It forms a neat mound eight inches high and covers itself with bell-shaped flowers of brilliant blue. For a pleasing display plant with it the variegated form of the old-fashioned *Arabis* and between them plant *Lilium maculatum* or *Tritonia crocata*.

Another plant of great beauty, which will be in bloom throughout summer, is *Prunella* 'Loveliness' which bears its thick spikes of clearest mauve-pink on nine-inch stems. Also long flowering is *Veronica* 'Shirley Blue', with spikes of gentian-blue on twelve-inch stems.

Where compact plants are required to act as a ground cover as well as supplying colour, use the dainty Violettas, their tiny Viola-like blooms on six-inch stems; they will be at their best when the Winter-flowering Violas are losing some of their brightness. The Violettas may be planted with the most diminutive bulbs and they will

82

remain neat and compact for several years, being increased by root division.

Even though less labour saving than perennials, annuals may be sown among the bulbs in April. As the seed germinates and the plants make growth, they will soon hide the unsightly foliage of the spring-flowering bulbs as it turns yellow and dies back, for it must be remembered that the foliage must not be removed until it has died down completely; otherwise the bulbs will soon lose vigour. An alternative method of hiding the unsightly foliage of the bulbs will be to press the foliage, as it turns brown and dies down, beneath the perennials.

There are many summer-flowering annuals which prefer to be sown where they are to bloom. The seed should be sown between the bulbs as soon as the soil becomes friable again after the winter. Scatter the seed over the surface and rake it in among the bulbs, using a child's rake or hand fork. A long-flowering and graceful annual to sow in early April is *Collinsia bicolor* 'Salmon Beauty', with masses of salmon-pink flowers on twelve-inch stems throughout summer. *Brachycome iberidifolia* is also well worth having, the 'Blue Star' hybrids bearing brilliant blue flowers from the end of June until October. It is only half-hardy, so delay sowing until early May. The Eschscholtzias, 'Dazzler' and 'Enchantress' prefer a dry soil and full sun and will bloom all summer, likewise the new dwarf Godetias, 'Lavender Queen' and 'Crimson Glow'. An unusual annual is *Layia elegans* 'Tidy Tips', flowering during August and September on ten-inch stems. Its dainty yellow flowers are tipped with white. *Phlox Drummondii*, night-scented Stock and the Nasturtium are also most attractive and will grow quickly from seed. Or plant, from boxes, Tagetes and dwarf French marigolds which will be already in bloom when planted out early in May and will remain in bloom until October. Likewise, 'Tom Thumb' Antirrhinums and Petunias. In late September, after the plants have flowered, they should be pulled up and the surface should be lightly forked over to a depth of one inch so as not to disturb the bulbs, for those which bloom early will already be pushing new leaves through the soil.

Anemones for bedding

An outstanding display may be obtained from April until late in autumn, and indeed in a sheltered garden the odd blooms will appear throughout the winter, from a planting of Anemones. These are grown in vast quantities as cut flowers but are rarely used for bedding display. For filling small beds there is no easier plant to manage, nor one that gives more flowers for the cost of the tubers. But the 'Poppy Anemone', well known to Elizabethan gardeners, and described in detail by Parkinson in his *Paradisus*, is neglected. Gardeners seem to think that because out-of-season bloom is produced in Cornwall it is a plant too tender for the rest of the country. The Elizabethan gardeners knew it to be fairly hardy, and they would have been in no way surprised if told that the poppy anemone grows to perfection as far north as the Shetland Isles; in fact it is thoroughly happy in the soot-laden soils of our towns and cities. When these qualities of hardiness are realized the Anemone will be planted in large numbers.

Another misapprehension is that a large corm will ensure bigger and better quality blooms than a small-sized one. This is so with all other bulbs, but with the Anemone, the reverse is the case; and whereas those old horned corms, so acclimatized to the fields of Holland (where they may have been grown for several years for the bloom) will have lost vigour, the tiny 2–3 cm. corms (tubers really) will provide a mass of large, brilliantly-coloured blooms. Corms larger than 3–4 cm. should not be used, for their vigour will have been lost in direct ratio to increase in size; also, the smaller the corm, the less expensive it will be.

One of the most attractive displays it has been my privilege to enjoy was of a large raised circular bed, in the dappled shade of young ornamental trees, consisting of circles of 'de Caen' and 'St. Brigid' anemones arranged in about a dozen separate colours. With their light feathery foliage, and flowers to be counted on from early summer until the autumn, the display was long-lasting and provided colour both in the garden and in the home. As Anemones resent disturbance, it is not possible to plant them among other bulbs, which might bloom earlier, and the lifting of which would harm the Anemone corms. In order to prolong the display of anemone blooms, the centre portions of a bed may be planted in early autumn and the outer portions in late March. In this way there would be flowers from mid-April until mid-October with no changing of the plants as would occur when spring and summer bedding plants are used. As an edging to a path or border they will retain their brilliance over a much longer period than will Pinks, Catmint or any of the other popular edging plants.

There are three important points to remember when growing anemones:

(i) They like a soil retentive of moisture.

(ii) They do not like a soil in any way acid.

(iii) They must not be planted too close together.

In preparing the bed, as much humus as possible should be added if the soil is of a light nature, decayed manure, peat, spent hops, anything to retain moisture during a dry period, for the Anemone will die back in a spell of drought. In fact, contrary to popular belief, the Anemone will grow better in a heavy soil, well drained, than in a light sandy soil. Wool shoddy is also excellent for Anemones, the plants benefiting from the slowly released nitrogen; wood ashes are also valuable for potash; or give a 2-oz. per square yard dressing of sulphate of potash to build up a hardy plant undamaged by cold winds (the Anemone's particular dislike).

As most town soils tend to be acid, hydrated lime should be added as the bed is prepared. Bone meal, too, should be included in small amounts, for it releases its food but slowly, an important consideration when it is remembered that the Anemone blooms over a very long period which may be prematurely terminated if the food supply becomes exhausted. Before planting, bring the soil to as fine a tilth as possible and allow it several days to settle down. This is so that the corms will make thorough contact with the soil: air pockets cause the roots to die back.

Distance and depth of planting are more important with Anemones than with any other bulbous plant. There is a tendency to set the tiny corms close together, like sown peas, but Anemones make masses of fibrous roots which will strangle each other if not given sufficient room. Plant five inches apart and two inches deep, and when the soil is friable with early spring planting, which is the general time for summer display, the beds should be trodden lightly and then raked level. There is nothing to be gained by planting before the soil begins to warm up; in the more favourable districts mid-March planting may be done, in the colder north, early April is soon enough. And always plant with a trowel rather than with a dibber.

The corms will be seen to have germinated after about five weeks and will be in bloom, in favourable weather, in eight weeks, by early June from a late March planting. The greatest care must be taken with weeding, for the roots will tend to die back if made loose. If hand weeding has to be done, then do it with care, pressing back any plants which may have been disturbed. Better than weeding is to give a mulch with peat before the plants make too much growth. Through periods of drought, the beds should be kept thoroughly moist. Each of these little details contribute to a long, colourful display.

Apart from the numerous reliable mixture of both the 'St. Brigids', which are double, and the single 'de Caens', there are a number of excellent named varieties. In singles, 'Hollandia' is vivid scarlet; 'Sylphide', soft magenta-pink; 'Gertrude', strawberry-pink; and 'The Bride', white with a black centre. In doubles, 'The Governor' is pillar-box red; 'Lord Lieutenant', navy blue; 'Queen of Brilliance', cherry-red; and 'The Admiral', violet-pink. Plant also *Anemone fulgens*, the starry 'Windflower of the Pyrenees'. The tubers may be obtained for about a guinea a hundred, and what a striking plant it is! The semi-double blooms are borne on nine-inch stems and are of dazzling scarlet with a blue-black centre; the elegant foliage is brilliant green.

The 'St. Bavo' Anemone is equally lovely and this strain may be obtained in glorious 'art' shades unobtainable in any other strain. For bedding, these must be numbered amongst the finest of all garden plants.

The Ranunculus

It is difficult to know just what to say about the Ranunculus in the modern garden. True, it blooms on stems of less than twelve inches and so would come within the range of plants described in this book, and without a doubt it is one of the finest of all garden plants. It is not difficult to understand the great esteem in which the plant was held by Victorian gardeners, and indeed by gardeners throughout the nineteenth century, but the corms are slightly tender and the flowering period covers barely a month, from the end of May until the last days of June. True, it blooms at a most difficult period in the garden, but it does interfere with planting for summer display, for the plants should be safely in their flowering quarters by the time the Ranunculus comes into bloom. A compromise may be made by lifting the Ranunculus immediately after flowering, and with the foliage intact, keeping the tubers in boxes of dry peat until the foliage has died down, when the tubers are cleaned and stored until ready for planting again. It should be said that whereas the Anemone is perfectly hardy in all parts of the British Isles, the Ranunculus will grow best south of a line drawn from Bristol to London; though there may be some latitude in this respect if the soil is thoroughly drained and the bed is protected from cold winds.

There are several strains of *Ranunculus asiaticus*, but today the Persian, French and Turban or Turkish are most popular. This is one of the old florist's flowers and so was taken up by enthusiasts in most parts of Europe; and the strains took on the district or country of their raisers. All grow to a height of nine to ten inches and the only distinct difference between each strain is that some, such as the Persian and Turkish, are fully double while others, including the Giant French strains, are semi-double, thus showing the central black boss which is so effective.

Persian and Turban Ranunculi are generally planted in late autumn, while the others seem to prefer an early March planting; but it must be said that where the soil is of a heavy, cold nature or the plants are to be grown in an exposed district, it is better to delay the planting of all strains until mid-March, otherwise the corms may decay. The Ranunculus enjoys a well-drained soil, one containing plenty of grit or sharp sand, yet at the same time the plants must never be allowed to suffer from drought, so should be given a soil enriched with decayed manure, old mushroom-bed compost or hop manure, which is augmented by decayed leaves or some peat. Like the Anemone, the Ranunculus likes a firm soil, so the bed should be prepared several weeks in advance of planting, and William Robinson also suggests a beating down of the soil after the corms have been planted for about a month.

The corms are set claw downwards and two inches deep, no deeper, spaced about four inches apart. If possible, sprinkle them with sand to ensure thorough drainage while they are rooting. Again as with the Anemone, the corms must be kept growing, and so will require consistent applications of water in periods of drought. The foliage will appear after about five or six weeks and will come into bloom in another six weeks.

Multiflora begonias

Perhaps a very much more suitable plant for the small modern garden is the tuberous Begonia, known as the Multiflora begonia on account of the large numbers of small flowers is bears from early July until the end of Autumn. This is an easily-grown plant which thrives on plenty of moisture, and during the two particularly wet summers of 1957 and 1958, no bedding plant gave a better account of itself, wind and continuous rain in no way troubling it. Few gardeners know of it, and when seen in bloom its exotic appearance belies its robust constitution. It is, in fact, one of the easiest of all plants to grow well; and all it asks for is a soil containing humus in the form of peat, hops or leaf mould, together with a small quantity of decayed manure. Humus it must have, to see it through a dry summer.

Like most bulbous plants, the Multiflora begonia will tolerate partial shade and is quite happy growing in a town garden. All that it requires is for the tubers to be started into growth in boxes, either in a closed frame or greenhouse, or outdoors in a sunny position, where the boxes may be covered with a sheet of glass to help the tubers into growth more rapidly, and to protect them from night frost. The tubers may also be started in April in the sunny window of a warm living-room, moist peat being all that is necessary to start them into growth. The tubers are small, only 3–5 cm. in diameter and by planting closely together as many as four dozen may be planted in a normal sized seed box, though a 'kipper' box with its greaterdepth will be more suitable. Press the tubers into the peat, which should have been made thoroughly moist and quite firm. Do not cover the tuber in any way but make sure that the flat or upper portion is left exposed, for this is where growth will take place. All that is necessary is to keep the peat comfortably moist, increasing the moisture as growth takes place. The plants should be gradually hardened towards the end of May, before planting out in prepared beds during the first days of June.

The plants should be set out nine inches apart, for they make bushy growth. Sempervivums look most attractive where used to surround a bed of Begonias or even planted among them. The Begonias should be set out with care so that neither the roots nor the rather brittle stems are damaged. They should be well watered in and at all times should be kept quite moist, otherwise bud-drop may result. After flowering the plants should be lifted and placed in a dry room for the foliage to die back gradually, when it is rubbed from the tuber. The tubers are then placed in boxes of dry peat for storing until required for starting into growth again in April. Treated with respect, they should remain vigorous for many years.

It is just fifty years since Messrs. Lemoine's of France introduced the first Multiflora begonias by crossing *Begonia octopetala* with a tuberous hybrid of unknown origin. There are now many lovely varieties which may either be planted in separate colours or as several varieties of contrasting colours together. The small blooms appear on short branching stems held above the handsome pointed bottle-green foliage and renew themselves in succession throughout summer and autumn. The satin-pink flowering 'Madelon' combines well with the crimson-red 'Count Zeppelin'; and 'His Excellency', of double orange-scarlet blooms, with the apricot-flowered 'Jewel', which has attractive dark green foliage. There are many more, all equally beautiful, and their culture presents no difficulties.

CHAPTER 8

The Trough Garden

The advantage of a trough garden—Construction of a trough—Suitable plants for a trough—Indispensable bulbs—Carpeting plants—Care of the trough

---

The advantages of a trough garden

A delightful garden in miniature may be formed where there is only sufficient space on which to stand a trough. This may be placed anywhere so long as overhead moisture from a roof or trees cannot drip on to it, thus causing excess moisture to remain about the bulbs, causing them to decay in the soured soil. Under the overhanging eaves of a house a trough may be placed directly against a house wall, possibly beneath a window, from which the beauty of the bulbs may be enjoyed whatever the weather in much the same way as with a window box. A trough may be placed against the walls of a paved courtyard, or on a terrace or verandah, or on a flat roof. Here, the trough garden may be planted so that it will give colour throughout the year and may be enjoyed, without dirtying one's shoes, during all weathers.

Though there is nothing quite comparable to weathered stone for the trough garden, concrete will prove suitable where a stone trough cannot be obtained; and concrete has the advantage of being porous, so the soil will keep sweet for much longer, the roots and bulbs of the plants healthier.

Of whatever material the trough is to be constructed, it must be provided with a drainage hole, but where the stone is extremely thick, and this is not possible, ample drainage materials should be placed at the bottom before the trough is filled with compost.

Construction of a trough

The most satisfactory way of constructing a concrete trough is to make two boxes of timber which has been planed, making one about 1½ inches smaller in all dimensions. The smaller box will fit inside the other. For the base and walls of the trough mix up 2 parts of sand to 1 part of cement, adding sufficient water to make it into a paste that will 'pour', yet at the same time is not too 'sloppy'. The cement should be poured inside the larger box to a depth of 1½ inches, two large corks being held in position to provide the drainage holes. To reinforce the base and sides, a length of wire netting should be pressed into the cement mixture just before it begins to set, and this should extend almost to the top of the sides. A second piece of netting should be pressed into the mixture so that it extends up the other two sides in a similar way. Use 2-inch mesh netting, cutting the pieces to the exact measurements of the mould. Thus for a box 20 inches long by 18 inches wide by 6 inches deep, the two pieces of netting will measure 42 inches and 30 inches. The smaller box does not require a base; just make the four sides and hold them together by small pieces of wood nailed across each corner and long enough to stretch across the corners of the first box to prevent it pressing into the concrete base. The cement is then poured between the two boxes. Insert a piece of stick to hold the netting away from the mould and this will prevent it showing when the concrete has finally set hard, which it will do in about twenty-four hours if not made too thin. Just before the cement has set completely, the sides of the boxes are carefully removed, the inner mould being left in position until all is thoroughly hardened. The wooden base and the corks are then pressed off.

Troughs are extremely heavy, so of whatever material they are constructed, they should be in their permanent sites before they are prepared for the plants. Make certain that they are quite firm on the single or double pedestal, using wedges where necessary. Over the drainage holes place several large crocks, or pieces of brick or stone, then over the whole base place a layer of small stones or crocks to a depth of six inches. Over this lay old turves upside down and then fill to the top with the prepared soil mixture, pressing it well down round the sides. This should be composed of:

2 parts fresh loam, sterilized if possible;
1 part top grade peat, which is superior to leaf mould because it contains no weed seeds;
1 part coarse sand and grit.

Add a sprinkling of superphosphate to encourage root action, and lime to keep it sweet; also give a little bone meal, a slow-acting fertilizer, and mix the whole together. If one has no garden, sterilized loam, peat and sand may readily be obtained from a local nursery; and as a general guide, a barrowful of compost will be required for a sink of approximately 36 inches by 18 inches by 6 inches. Most stone troughs are several inches deeper, but rarely more than 24–26 inches in length, so that compost requirements will be much the same. Some troughs have no drainage holes and so should be given a greater depth of material to assist in their drainage, while some pieces of broken charcoal should be mixed with the compost to maintain its sweetness.

Suitable plants for a trough

Where more than one trough can be made up, it will be possible to confine to one those plants which enjoy plenty of lime in the soil, such as the dwarf Alpine pinks, a number of the Saxifrages and Sempervivums. *Androsace sempervivoides*, which bears umbels of pink flowers during April, loves lime and will often be in bloom at the same time as those other lime lovers, *Iris reticulata* and *Cyclamen coum* and *C. repandum*. *Aethionema iberideum*, the Persian Candy-tuft, also likes a dry, chalky soil, its ash-grey foliage and white flowers acting as a pleasing foil to the April-flowering crocuses and irises. There are also later-flowering forms of these delightful alpine plants to extend the season. A trough may be made up with those plants enjoying a moist, peaty soil such as the extremely dwarf *Juliae* primroses 'F. Ashby', with its tiny claret red blooms, and 'Snow Cushion'. The tiny heather, 'Mrs. Ronald Gray', which forms a small prostrate clump one inch high and is covered with deep purple bells in September, and 'Mrs. Pat', which blooms in spring, are ideal plants for a peaty soil; and besides being good to look at, will prevent the tiny blooms of the bulbs from being splashed. The lovely *Cassiope lycopodioides*, a shrublet of the heather family which bears masses of tiny white bells during May, is also suitable. For planting in a trough containing a peaty soil, and where situated in partial shade, the Dog's Tooth Violets, with their pretty mottled foliage and dainty rosy-mauve blooms, are quite delightful, very similar in form to the hardy cyclamen. The Snowdrops and Winter Aconite will also do well in such a soil.

Where the trough is in full sunshine, among those plants suitable for such a situation will be the Androsace, Aubrieta, *Asperula Gussoni, Helianthemum alpestre* and *Veronica Halleri*. Each of these plants, with the exception of the Aubrieta which is useful for planting to trail over the sides, is of dwarf, shrubby habit, thereby affording protection to the miniature bulbs as they come into bloom. For a sun-baked position, the most suitable bulbs are the irises; *Anomatheca cruenta*, which bears its salmon-orange flowers on four-inch stems during July and August; *Brodiaea minor*, having tiny umbels of deepest blue during June; and the crocuses. Also, where the trough is in a sheltered, sunny position, do not forget *Rhodohypoxis baurii*, with pink flowers, two-inch stems and attractive grey leaves.

Bulbs for a trough garden should be of pronouncedly dwarf habit, and those which tend to increase rapidly, whether from seed or by the formation of bulblets, should be omitted, for they will tend to crowd out their neighbours. The bulbs should not grow more than six inches tall, and their foliage should remain neat and tidy after flowering. This rule will exclude a number of the dwarf Tulips, the Colchicums and dwarf Alliums which would be suitable in all other respects.

The best effect will be obtained by making the trough into a tiny alpine garden complete with tufa stone and miniature trees. Just two or three pieces of stone should be used, placed well down into the soil and in the same way as recommended for a garden rockery, so as to give the stone a natural appearance, the grain at a slight slope and in the same direction for each piece of stone. About the stones one or possibly two miniature trees should be planted to give the trough a garden-like appearance, and none is more suitable than the tiny Balsam Fir or the dwarf Norway Spruce *Picea excelsa nana compacta*. Both are broader than they are tall, and they rarely exceed five inches. Then add a few dwarf alpine plants as suggested, to provide protection for the bulbs and to give colour over as long a period as possible, often when the bulbs will not be in bloom. Between these plants the bulbs will be planted in groups of two or three.

Indispensable bulbs

Indispensable bulbs for a trough garden are the Chionodoxas: not *C. gigantea* which is rather too robust, but *C. luciliae* (brilliant blue) and *rosea* (delicate pink). There is also a beautiful white form, *alba*.

The daintiest of the crocuses are suitable, three bulbs being planted close together, almost touching, for best effect. To flower in October:

C. asturicus, pale mauve; and for November: *C. ochroleucus*, creamy white; for February: *C. Fleischeri* and *C. ancyrensis*. The Hardy cyclamen, which blooms in autumn, is an excellent plant for trough culture. Its pale pink flowers, which look like moths, hover above the small rounded leaves. The foliage is enhanced by an attractive silver zone. The spring-flowering *C. coum* and *C. repandum* may also be used.

The most slender of the Grape Hyacinths, *Muscari azureum*, with its spikes of pale blue 'grapes', also its white counterpart, *alba*, do well in a trough, also the little *Scilla bifolia*, in its dark-blue and shell-pink form.

No trough garden will be complete without at least one of the Tulip species, though with most the foliage tends to grow rather too large for a trough. Suitable is the shining scarlet *T. Maximowiczii*, and *T. dasystemon*, which has several yellow flowers to each stem. Both flower in April, while for May *T. persica*, with its tiny yellow and bronze blooms held on only three-inch stems, is indispensable.

Of the miniature daffodils, *Narcissus minimus* and *N. minor*, the fragrant *N. juncifolius* and the dainty double flowered 'Wee Bee', are all suitable for a trough, but will not generally bloom in their first season.

A rare little bulbous plant of great beauty is the Pyrenean Meadow Saffron, *Merendera sobolifera*. Its fragile cups of palest pink on three-inch stems begin to appear early in April and these are followed by dark green leaves which are so neat as to make this plant one which may be thoroughly recommended for trough garden and rockery.

Another gem, in bloom throughout spring, and equally at home on the rockery, is *Fritillaria pudica*. A native of Western North America, it is quite hardy. It likes a sunny position and is best planted in a pocket of sand, for the bulbs will decay with an excess of winter moisture. On four- to five-inch stems it has four or five nodding bells of purest gold, a most brilliant sight in the spring sunshine.

When the leaves begin to die down after the bulbs have flowered, anything but the neatest foliage will be unsightly for long periods. Bulbs having upright, grass-like leaves will never be too conspicuous, as they turn brown; and if carpeting plants are used as freely as space permits, the leaves will be even less noticeable, as they grow through the carpeters.

Carpeting plants

The bulbs should be planted so that as they spread, they may grow up through the carpeters, obtaining support, shelter and protection from soil splashing. This last, however, may also be prevented by covering the soil around the plants with spar chippings, which will set off the flowers to perfection and will also suppress weeds until the carpeters have covered the trough.

So valuable are carpeting plants for use with miniature bulbs, not only in the trough garden but also about the alpine garden, that a list of suitable plants may prove helpful.

Name	Foliage	Flowers
Acaena Buchanani	Glaucous-green	—
„ *inermis*	Purple-Bronze	—
Arenaria caespitosa aurea	Golden	White
„ *purpurescens*	Purple	White
Armeria caespitosa	Green	Pink
Asperula lilaciflora	Emerald-green	Pink
Campanula 'E. H. Frost'	Bright green	White
„ *pulla lilacina*	Bright green	Lilac/Rose
Cotula species	Purple-Green	—
Draba bryoides imbricata	Grey-green	Yellow
„ *pyrenaica*	Dark green	Mauve
Frankenia thymaefolia	Grey-green	Pink
Globularia bellidifolia	Bottle-green	Blue
Hippocrepis 'E. R. Janes'	Bottle-green	Lemon
Houstonia coerulea	Bottle-green	Blue
Linaria aequitriloba	Dark green	Mauve
Lippia repens	Grey-green	Pink
Nierembergia rivularis	Dark green	White
Raoulia australis	Silver	Yellow
„ *lutescens*	Grey	Golden
Saxifraga oppositifolia splendens	Emerald	Crimson
Sedum acre minor	Bronze	Yellow
„ *dasyphyllum*	Glaucous-green	White
„ *hispanicum aureum*	Gold	White
„ *lydium*	Green, turning scarlet	Yellow
Silene acaulis saxatilis	Emerald	Pink
Thymus nieciffii	Silver-grey	Cerise
„ *Serpyllum minus*	Grey-green	Pink
Wahlenbergia serpyllifolia	Dark green	Purple

THE TROUGH GARDEN

With their mat-like foliage taking on almost every conceivable colouring possible in plant foliage, many remaining in bloom from spring until autumn, the carpeting plants may be said to be indispensable for planting with the tiniest of the miniature bulbs.

These are the most suitable miniature bulbs to grow with them in the trough garden:

Name	Flowering Time	Height
Anomatheca cruenta	July–August	4–5 ins.
Chionodoxa luciliae	March–April	4 ins.
„ *sardensis*	March–April	4 ins.
Crocus ancyrensis	Feb.–March	2 ins.
„ *asturicus*	Oct.–Nov.	4 ins.
„ *candidus*	April	2 ins.
„ *Korolkowi*	Sept.–Oct.	1½ ins.
„ *laevigatus*	Dec.–Feb.	3 ins.
„ *minimus*	March–April	1½ ins.
„ *ochroleucus*	Nov.–Dec.	2 ins.
„ *olivieri*	April–May	2 ins.
„ *sativus*	Oct.–Nov.	2 ins.
„ *zonatus*	Sept.–Oct.	4 ins.
Cyclamen alpinum	Dec.–Feb.	3 ins.
„ *coum*	Jan.–April	3 ins.
Erythronium dens-canis	March–April	5–6 ins.
„ *Hendersonii*	March–April	4 ins.
Fritillaria pudica	April–May	4 ins.
Hyacinthus dalmaticus	April–May	4 ins.
Iris Danfordiae	February	3–4 ins.
„ *reticulata*	March–April	5–6 ins.
Merendera sobolifera	April–May	3 ins.
Narcissus juncifolius	April	4 ins.
„ *minimus*	Feb.–March	4 ins.
„ *Watieri*	May	4 ins.
„ 'Wee Bee'	April	4 ins.
Puschkinia scilloides	March–May	4 ins.
Rhodohypoxis baurii	May–June	3 ins.
Romulea sabulosa	May–July	3 ins.
Scilla verna	March–April	4 ins.
Tulipa Batalini	March–April	4 ins.
„ *biflora*	March–April	5 ins.

24. *Crocus chrysanthus.* 'Bluebird'. An outstanding variety of large, sturdy growth. Outer petals deep aster blue with a white margin. When fully open the vivid orange stamens are very attractive to bees

25. *Crocus chrysanthus.* 'Snowbunting'

26. *Chionodoxa luciliae*, 'Glory of the Snow'

27. *Crocus Sieberi*. 'Hubert Edelsten'

28. *Crocus ancyrensis*. 'Goldenbunch Crocus'. Spring flowering (January)

29. *Narcissus cyclamineus*. Hybrid 'Peeping Tom'

Name	Flowering Time	Height
Tulipa dasystemon	April–May	6 ins.
„ *persica*	May	3 ins.
„ *pulchella*	March–April	4 ins.
„ *Wilsoniana*	May	3 ins.

Bear in mind that if your trough is to be a colourful feature all the year round, you must plant for a succession.

Care of the trough

Where the soil is well drained and the surface is covered with spar chippings or with carpeting plants, there will be little fear of moss forming. This would quickly choke the alpine plants, though bulbs would not be troubled in the same degree. It is also important to guard against dripping from trees or eaves which would cause the soil to 'pan', thus depriving the plants of the necessary oxygen.

As the alpine plants will be pot grown, they may be set out at almost any time except when the soil is frozen or may be excessively wet. The best time to make up a trough, however, will be in the early weeks of autumn, when the spring and summer flowering bulbs should be planted. First plant the dwarf trees and any suitable alpine plants which will serve to prevent an over-flat appearance. Then plant the carpeters and any plants that are to trail over the sides, finally inserting the bulbs in small groups almost anywhere. Let them push up through the carpeters and other plants, but do plant so that they will produce colour the whole year round. Also, leave a few spaces for the autumn- and winter-flowering bulbs which can be planted during June, setting them close to those bulbs which will have bloomed early so as to hide the dead foliage. The trough garden will take fully twelve months to become established but afterwards there will be a continuous display for the minimum of trouble.

During dry weather, the plants will require watering, sometimes as often as twice a day, while the plants will appreciate an occasional syringeing with cold, clean water. Never water while the sun remains on the plants for fear of scorching the foliage. Nightfall is the best time, and make sure that the soil is thoroughly soaked or the roots will turn to the surface in search of moisture.

Town-grown plants often end the winter coated with grime from fogs. This may be removed by spraying with tepid water into which a pinch of Wetting Compound has been mixed: the compound enables the water to remain on the foliage to do its work of cleaning. Warm and gentle spring rains will soon give a new look to the trough garden, and as the sun gathers strength, more and more bulbs will begin to flower.

At the end of each winter stir up the surface soil as gently as possible, adding a little decayed manure which has been finely screened. At the same time, remove the dead foliage of those plants which flowered in autumn and press soil around the roots of any plants made loose by hard frost.

Both the carpeting plants and the bulbs will need cutting back and dividing after a time, and so that the display will be maintained, a few clumps of bulbs should be lifted and divided each year. Lift with care and wash away the soil before dividing and replanting the best as soon as possible after the foliage has died down.

To maintain vigour, remove all faded blooms without delay, but retain the foliage until it has turned brown. This will not be unsightly if later flowering bulbs and alpine plants are there to hide it.

The Sink Garden

Almost all those miniature flowering bulbs which are suitable for a trough garden may be grown in a sink. An old kitchen sink may be brought into suitable condition by first removing some of the glaze so that the plant's roots are able to anchor themselves to the surface. Drainage will usually be limited to the plug hole, and to ensure that it functions correctly, a ball of wire netting should be pressed inside before the drainage materials are added. If the sink is so wedged on to its pedestal that there is a slight fall towards the plug end, surplus moisture caused by heavy rain will drain away.

To assist with the drainage, a layer of broken crocks should be placed over the base, on top of which should lie some shingle. Then add a layer of turf loam and fill up the sink with compost as recommended for a trough garden. As there will not be so great a depth of compost in a sink, this should be as rich as possible, incorporating a larger proportion of decayed manure than for a trough compost.

Small pieces of tufa stone may be used to provide as realistic an effect as possible, and about these the most dainty of the bulbs, and those alpine plants of almost prostrate habit, may be planted. Care should be taken with a sink garden to ensure that during dry weather the plants do not lack moisture.

CHAPTER 9

Bulbs for the Window Box

The idea of replacement boxes—Constructing a window box—Preparing the box—Bulbs suitable for a window box

D warf bulbs are ideal for window boxes, as they are not only low growing, which makes them able to withstand strong winds, but are also inexpensive and colourful. Boxes of similar dimensions may also be fixed to the wall of a courtyard for almost year-long display.

The idea of replacement boxes

Here I would like to make a suggestion for a procedure which will greatly prolong the display. If additional boxes are planted with dwarf bulbs either at the same time as the original box, or in spring for bulbs to bloom in autumn, and if the boxes have been so constructed that they will fit inside the permanent window box, the display may be extended for many weeks. The permanent box may be planted with bulbs and plants which may be expected to bloom during the latter part of winter and early spring, including the Crocus species, *Iris reticulata*, the Chionodoxas and Winter aconites, the Winter-flowering polyanthus 'Barrowby Gem', and the Winter-flowering violas. When the fixed box is planted in November, prepare also additional box (or boxes) to act as replacement when the early bulbs and plants have finished flowering at the end of April.

The replacement box may be planted with tulips of all types but particularly with the colourful *T. Kaufmanniana* hybrids such as 'Gluck', 'Robert Schumann' and 'Shakespeare', which bear their large globular blooms on six-inch stems. Other good tulips are *T. Fosteriana* 'Princeps', *T. Greigii* and *T. Kolpakowsiana* which come into flower at the end of April or in May. Other possibilities for the replacement box are the Alpine Hyacinths, Plume Hyacinth, and

99

the related Grape Hyacinths, 'Heavenly Blue' and 'Cantab'; or perhaps the late-flowering miniature daffodils, and very late-flowering crocuses. Do not forget that the miniature daffodils resent disturbance, and when used in this way should be retained for several years. The Tulips, Irises and Crocuses will do well in dry, sunny conditions, but if the box is to be fixed in a cold, sunless position, plant the Snowdrops, Daffodils and Scillas.

After the earliest-flowering bulbs have been removed, the replacement boxes are put into position, and after their bulbs have finished flowering at the end of May, the boxes are removed intact to a shaded corner (even to the cellar or attic) where the bulbs are allowed to die down gradually, just as they would if growing in the open ground. They should not be disturbed in any way, though the foliage should be removed later in the year. Where the boxes have been kept under cover they should be exposed to the elements again at the approach of winter. At the same time, the boxes may be topped up with fresh compost and covered with ashes. The bulbs will come into growth again the following spring and the buds will have formed by the time the boxes are ready for replacement in April.

A well-prepared compost in the first instance, and watering with dilute liquid manure for several weeks immediately after the bulbs have flowered, will maintain them in a vigorous condition for several years without removal from the box or replacement of soil. Geraniums and Salvias, or other half-hardy summer plants, could follow in a second replacement box early in June. The plants will be thoroughly established when introduced to the fixture box and will come into bloom without delay. By this method the boxes will be continuously colourful, whilst it is a much simpler matter to prepare a box before placing it in position. What is more, the fixed box will enjoy a very much longer life where it is not in direct contact with moist soil. I make no apologies for describing this method at some length for many a city dweller who has no garden can enjoy window box gardening by the replacement method. Those who have a small backyard may grow boxes of flowers in exactly the same way, and here the replacement boxes will be more easily prepared and managed.

If the provision of box after box is not practicable, bulbs which are dying back may be replaced by later-flowering bulbs, grown separately in small pots. They should be planted in autumn, and must be allowed several months in the plunge bed, or in a cellar or darkened room, to enable them to form a strong rooting system; they should then be moved to a cool place where the light is partly diffused and where they will continue to make growth, but slowly. The pots may go into the window box at the appropriate time either as replacements for all the early flowering bulbs or as replacements for individual plants as these die down. The pot rims should be just covered with soil. At the end of May the pots may be removed together with any other bulbs of the original planting, so that the boxes may be replanted for the summer display. It will not be necessary to remove the bulbs from the pots each year and with those bulbs which resent disturbance, e.g. the Dwarf daffodils, it is harmful.

Bulbs will be indispensable for window boxes, since they are better able to withstand severe weather than ordinary plants, and will put up a brave show even in sunless positions. Hard frosts and strong winds which tend to dry out the compost will have little effect on the bulbs provided there is an ample depth of compost in which their roots may penetrate. The deeper the box, and the better the compost, the less labour will there be, for well-prepared compost will not dry out too quickly during periods of drought; indeed, in certain seasons the bulbs may never require watering or much attention of any kind.

Constructing a window box

As a window box has to carry a considerable weight of soil, it should be constructed of 1-inch wood, cut to the correct lengths and planed. The front and back of the box should be cut to the total length required, as the ends will be fixed inside. When cutting the ends, allow for the thickness of front and back so as to keep to the correct overall measurements required. If any attempt is made to dovetail the corners it should be remembered that the strength of a dovetail lies in the perfection of its construction and a water-resistant glue should be used. Always bear in mind that a good, simple job is better than a bad complicated one. When securing the two ends no advantage will be gained by using screws instead of 2-inch nails. For additional strength at the corners an angle bracket should be screwed either on the inside or outside of the box.

Adequate drainage holes should be made in the base; a dozen or so holes of $\frac{1}{2}$-inch diameter are better than half the number of 1-inch diameter, since larger holes allow too much compost to dribble away. Where possible, use hard wood, such as seasoned oak, or failing that,

American Red Cedar, both of which will remain almost impervious to moisture through the years and neither of which requires painting as a preservative. A depth of six inches is enough for small bulbs.

After the box has been made up it should be treated on the inside with a wood preservative, say Cuprinol. This treatment is especially necessary if the box has been constructed of deal or other soft wood. Thoroughly soak the inside of the box and then leave it in the open for at least ten days for weathering; by the end of that time, any fumes which might be injurious to plant life will have escaped. The box may then be painted on the outside only.

The correct fixing of the box is all-important and must be governed by the structure. A window with a wooden frame will present few difficulties if the box is made to the exact dimensions of the frame. In this case, a strong iron bracket may be fixed to the top of the sides of the box, spanning the thickness of both front and back pieces, and to the frame of the window, and this should be quite secure. Security is most important for it must be remembered that a window box filled with soil is of considerable weight, especially when the soil is wet. Falling soil is a source of danger which must be guarded against. There must be no interference with the normal means of opening and closing the window, and ease of watering and planting of the box must be assured. Owing to the considerable weight of a filled box, it should of course be fixed into position when empty, then filled either from inside or outside.

Where a box has to be fixed to a stone or brick wall, the wall must first be plugged to a depth of not less than 2 inches for screw-holes. To give added efficiency to the fixture, strong galvanized wires should be fastened from the outer edge of the box sides to a position on the wall above the bracket. This will take some of the strain of a box which may have become unduly heavy through continuous rains or a fall of snow.

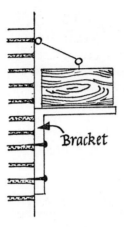

Bracket

The inner box to be used as a replacement should be constructed of ¾-inch timber, and though it should be treated with preservative, it will not require painting. At the top edge of each side of the box metal handles should be firmly screwed on to make insertion and lifting a simple matter. Before removing a box in which bulbs are growing, allow the soil to become as dry as possible, for as little as half a gallon of water weighs five pounds.

Preparing the box

Before placing any compost in the boxes it will be necessary to ensure thorough drainage. First the drainage holes in the base must be made, and in order to prevent wastage of soil you should lay a piece of fine mesh wire netting over the base. Then add a layer of crocks to a depth of about half an inch to ensure efficient drainage during winter. Over the crocks, a layer of turves placed grass downwards will occupy another one-and-a-half inches of the box. The remaining space is filled with prepared compost.

The soil in the compost mixture should preferably be taken from pasture, or be a good quality loam from a country garden not troubled by deposits of soot and sulphur. Soil taken from a town garden will generally be acid and full of weed seeds. A satisfactory compost will be made up by mixing:

3 parts loam;
1 part peat;
1 part grit or coarse sand (by weight).

Allow 2 lb. of ground limestone or lime rubble to a box 3 ft. long and 6 inches deep; 4 oz. of bone meal (a slow-acting fertilizer) and a sprinkling of superphosphate which encourages vigorous root action. Or as an alternative, the John Innes Compost, obtainable from most nurseryman, may be used.

The compost should be allowed a few days to settle down before any planting is done; and to prevent loss of compost over the sides when the boxes are watered, or during periods of heavy rain, leave about ¾ inch space between the top of the compost and the top of the box. In any case, always water with care so as not to cause splashing; and when the compost appears to be dry on the surface, give sufficient water to penetrate right through the compost so that the roots of the plants need not come up in search of it.

The bulbs should be planted at depths approximating to those in the open ground, but closer together, with no more than an inch between them. They should be planted in groups of three or four rather than as odd bulbs placed here and there about the box.

To keep the boxes tidy, the flowers should be removed as they fade; since replacement boxes are to be used, the unsightliness of dying-back foliage will not be one of your worries.

Bulbs suitable for a window box

Name	Flowering Time	Height
Begonia multiflora	June–Oct.	6–8 ins.
Brodiaea crocea	May–June	6 ins.
Chionodoxa gigantea	April	5 ins.
Crocus chrysanthus	Feb.–April	4 ins.
,, Dutch Hybrids	March–April	5 ins.
,, *imperati*	Jan.–March	3 ins.
,, *Karduchorum*	Sept.–Oct.	4 ins.
,, *niveus*	Dec.–March	4 ins.
Galanthus Elwesii	March–April	8 ins.
,, *nivalis*	Feb.–March	5 ins.

BULBS FOR THE WINDOW BOX

Name	Flowering Time	Height
Hyacinthus amethystinus	March–April	8 ins.
„ *azureus*	April	5 ins.
Iris reticulata	March–April	6 ins.
Muscari, 'Heavenly Blue'	March–April	6 ins.
„ *Tubergenianum*	April–May	9 ins.
Narcissus cyclamineus	March–April	9 ins.
„ *odorus*	May	8 ins.
„ 'Rip van Winkle'	March	6 ins.
„ *tenuior*	May–June	9 ins.
Scilla sibirica	Feb.–April	8 ins.
Tulipa Eichleri	April	10 ins.
„ *Fosteriana* 'Princeps'	April–May	8 ins.
„ *Griegii*	April	9 ins.
„ *Hageri*	April	9 ins.
„ *Kaufmanniana*	March–April	8–10 ins.
„ *Tubergeniana*	May	10 ins.

CHAPTER 10

Bulbs in the Home

Indoor bulbs of great beauty—The treatment of indoor bulbs—The plunge bed—Bulbs in bowls

---

Indoor bulbs of great beauty

Those bulbs which may be classed as true miniatures will be far more attractive in the small room of country cottage or town flat and will require considerably less attention by way of staking and tying than those of more robust habit. On my desk as I write are two earthenware pans in one of which is growing the dainty *Iris reticulata* in numerous varieties. The blooms possess a richness of colour and a fragrance not to be found in any other indoor bulb. The flowers stand well displayed on straight six-inch stems, their grass-like leaves almost clinging to the flower stems. It is late in February and the blooms have now been showing colour for several weeks and yet have not quite reached their best. A dozen bulbs of each of four different varieties have been planted together and there is not a single failure. Visitors often ask for their name, so rarely are these little gems seen growing. Yet they are adaptable and cheap.

In the second pan are growing the Dog's Tooth Violets, *Erythronium dens-canis*. They require a reasonably moist compost enriched with plenty of leaf mould, whereas the Irises enjoy a fairly poor soil containing some lime rubble. Indoors, in diffused light, Dog's Tooth Violets will stay in bloom for five or six weeks, the cyclamen-like flowers hovering like butterflies above the beautifully mottled foliage. The lovely *Erythronium californicum* 'White Beauty' may also be grown in pans indoors, though it grows taller. It, too, has richly mottled foliage, and bears its cream and chocolate zoned flowers on nine-inch stems. Both the Irises and the Dog's Tooth Violets bloom when the days are beginning to lengthen and there is a feeling of spring in the air, yet outside the winds blow cold and there is little

106

colour to be found except among the Snowdrops and Winter aconites. I know of no other bulbous plants which remain longer in flower than the Erythroniums and *Iris reticulata,* nor any more beautiful, and I should be sad to see my desk without them at this time of the year.

For early flowering, a few pots of Crocuses should be planted with the other bulbs in early September. The blooms will not remain colourful as long as the other plants I have mentioned, but they may be welcome all the same. Plant six corms to a 60-size pot, or nine to a pan or bowl. The neat orange and purple flowers of *C. candidus subflavus* remain fresh longer than those of any other Crocus. *C. Sieberi,* with blue flowers which have a striking golden throat, also does well in the home, and a pan filled with *Crocus chrysanthus* in half a dozen varieties will make a colourful show. Several of the more glamorous varieties should be grown because, indoors, they may be given extra attention and their blooms will remain clean and bright and should look as if they have been polished. An outstanding crocus is *C. chrysanthus* 'Zwanenburg Bronze', the exterior of the large golden yellow blooms is of rich bronze. Beautiful, too, is the *C. biflorus* seedling, 'Kittiwake', which has soft violet-blue petals margined with white.

Nor must the Winter aconites be neglected. As many as a dozen tubers should be planted in a large pan if one is to see them at their best. Plant *Eranthis hyemalis* indoors where it will bear its large golden cups in the dullest days of January. But the lovely 'Guinea Gold' is later to flower, with large golden blooms on short, bronze-coloured stems, and foliage that is also attractively tinted withbronze.

Snowdrops in small pots and Chionodoxas in pans are decorative during the dullest weeks of the year. The best method is to plant half a dozen bulbs of several species and varieties in a large seed pan. If they are taken indoors at the end of November, they will begin to bloom late in January, beginning with *C. sardensis.* They will continue to bloom until early April, always fresh and colourful. The appearance of the blooms will be greatly enhanced if the outside of the pan is covered with a piece of black material.

Indoor bulbs are best grown in porous earthenware pots or pans with ample drainage holes, as the compost remains sweet in such containers, and the degree of moisture-retention is satisfactory. Plastic and similar bowls will often lack drainage holes and are not porous. Earthenware containers are thought by some to be crude and undecorative; if you wish to do so, you could fix some kind of material around the containers when taken indoors, or place fresh moss over the compost between the plants, held in position with hairpins.

Perhaps no flower is more eagerly awaited than the Hyacinth, not only because it remains long in bloom but because its powerful fragrance is unique among indoor bulbs. It has been grown in England for just four hundred years, for it was in 1560 that Anthony Jenkinson introduced it from Persia. The bulbs have always remained expensive, since it is a plant that is slow to increase. For its propagation it requires a deep, sandy soil with a high water content, a condition which is to be found only in parts of Holland. Whereas the Early or Roman hyacinths and the later large-flowering varieties may not truly come within the scope of this book, the multi-flowering varieties and the early summer-flowering *H. amethystinus* are most dainty and graceful, and ideal subjects for growing in a small room.

The multi-flowered Hyacinths, like the 'Romans', bloom indoors during March. As the bulbs are small in comparison with those of the large-flowered varieties, they are best planted in earthenware bowls which will accommodate five or six bulbs. Several stems will be produced from each bulb, so that the frequently stark appearance we have come to associate with the large-flowered hyacinths need not be feared. The bulbs will stand up to quite hard forcing but will be happier where brought on gradually in a warm room; and like all members of the family they require copious amounts of moisture as the bulbs make growth. The bulbs should be given a period in the dark in which to form their roots, before being introduced to a warm room, otherwise the flower spikes will not be correctly formed. At all times the compost should be kept comfortably moist.

To follow the multi-flowered, choose 'Rosalie' with its loose, graceful spikes of rose-pink, and 'Vanguard', pale blue, planted either separately or together. A little later comes the many-flowered 'Borah', with its bells of porcelain blue, its fragrance will permeate a small house.

Of the Tulip species, *T. Kaufmanniana* and *T. Fosteriana* hybrids, with their huge, brilliantly-coloured blooms, are the ones most suitable for indoor culture. They will withstand quite warm conditions if they have been allowed to form a strong root run.

Treatment of indoor bulbs

Where growing bulbs indoors one must foresee the numerous pitfalls which may result in disappointment. There are two methods by which the bulbs may be brought into bloom: they may either be planted as bulbs or corms at the appropriate time, and after a period of darkness, during which they become well rooted, brought into a warm room; or for those with a garden, they may be lifted from the open ground as soon as plant growth appears above the soil, potted, and brought into bloom in a warm room. The latter method is the simplest, for by the time the plants are ready for lifting the flower buds will already have formed; and all that is required will be to complete the process by bringing them slowly along and keeping them comfortably moist about the roots. There need be nothing special about the compost, for the plants will occupy the pots for only a short time. Any friable compost will be suitable. The plants should be given a covering of dried leaves in early winter to provide protection against hard frost and to make it easier to lift them without causing damage as soon as plant growth can be seen.

It will generally be during the early days of February that the spring-flowering plants will be ready for lifting; and this will often be a time of hard frost. The plants may either be lifted individually or in small clumps and in this way the Snowdrops, Scillas, Dog's Tooth Violets, Miniature daffodils and Dwarf irises may be brought early into bloom. Remember, when lifting, that most of the bulbs planted outdoors will be from three to four inches deep, which means that it will be necessary to place the trowel quite six inches below the surface if vital rooting system is not to be harmed. Plants to be lifted in this way and taken indoors should not be subjected to any great degree of heat. The outdoor spring-flowering plants are extremely hardy and just will not tolerate forcing conditions. Until they have become re-established in the pots, the plants should be placed in an outhouse or washing room where they will remain for a week; then they may be taken indoors and placed in the window of a room that is not too warm. After flowering, the bulbs should be replanted into the same positions from which they were lifted and the same bulbs should not be taken indoors again for at least two years. This method will not, of course, be suitable for those living in a small town house or flat with little or no space for the growing of bulbs outdoors. In such cases, the bulbs must be planted in pots or earthenware bowls in early autumn and they will never see the open ground, unless maybe after they have bloomed, when they could be handed on to someone with a garden, to flower outdoors in the years to come.

The plunge bed

Those who have a small garden or courtyard will be able to root their bulbs outdoors in a plunge bed, and this is by far the most successful method. No bulb will give a really good account of itself unless it first builds up a sturdy rooting system, and this means that the bulb must be prevented from making top growth until it has formed its roots. Light must, therefore, be entirely excluded and this may be done either by placing the bulbs beneath a bed of ashes outdoors or in a cool, dark place indoors. The former method has much to recommend it, for where the pots or pans can be placed on a bed of ashes to encourage drainage, with a six-inch covering of ashes over the top to exclude light, the bulbs will be cool and may be kept thoroughly moist but not so moist that decay sets in. Where possible, the pots should be placed in ashes made firm, or preferably placed over a hard surface so that worms will not penetrate through to the pots. Sand or grit may be used as an alternative to ashes.

The fact that the plunge bed will be exposed to the elements until the end of November will mean that the bulbs will receive ample supplies of moisture, without which they will be unable to form a vigorous rooting system. This is the reason why there are so many failures with bulbs at all times confined indoors, where a dry cupboard or somewhere beneath the stairs will be the only available place in which to keep the bulbs in the dark. Much better would it be to place them beneath the kitchen or scullery sink away from the fire, for here the bulbs would be growing in a moister atmosphere. But wherever possible, make up a plunge bed outdoors even if no more than half a dozen pots are being grown, for the bulbs will receive ample supplies of moisture and remain cool. In such conditions they will build up a vigorous root run which will be seen through the drainage holes when the pots are removed from the plunge bed; and once in a warm room, the bulbs will be stimulated into growth without delay. The bulbs should be introduced to the light by degrees. First, the ashes should be shaken from the pots, which should be cleaned with a damp cloth before going indoors. There they should be placed in half light for several days, otherwise the foliage, which will have appeared already, may turn brown at the edges and so spoil what may well be a delightful display. If possible, where the plants are growing in the dry atmosphere of a room heated by a gas fire or by central heating, stand the pots or bowls in earthenware plant pot 'saucers', which are glazed on the inside and so may be kept filled with water.

At all times the compost should be kept comfortably moist; and as the plants make growth and come into bloom this will mean that more frequent waterings will be necessary. There can be no hard-and-fast rule as to watering; this must depend upon whether the pots are placed in a sunny window or one facing north; upon the compost used; and upon the heat of the room. Also, some bulbous plants will require considerably more moisture than others, Hyacinths especially. But do not conclude that the bulbs require moisture whenever the surface becomes dry, for lower down the compost may still be damp. First give the pot a tap with a piece of wood, and if there is a dull 'thud', water should be withheld until the tapping produces a more 'ringing' sound; then give a thorough soaking by watering round the side of the pots. To prevent plant growth from being drawn to the light, it will be advisable to turn the pots round a little each day. In this way foliage and flower stems will grow straight and sturdy.

Bulbs in bowls

Bulbs rooted in a plunge bed will rarely suffer from lack of moisture, neither should they be troubled by excess moisture remaining about the roots if the pots are well crocked and placed on a bed of ashes. But bulbs grown in bowls without drainage may suffer from both defects, with the result that the flowering display will prove disappointing. Where there is not adequate drainage, it is difficult to give just the correct amount of moisture for the bulbs to make vigorous root growth, yet without causing them to decay. Moisture is necessary to start the roots into growth and failure in this respect combined with a too warm atmosphere will stimulate the bulbs into early growth at the expense of root formation. Lack of moisture will cause stunting, the blooms being borne on too short a stem, which will greatly detract from the display. It is all too commonly believed that if the bulbs are placed in warmth as soon as they are planted in the bowls, they will come into bloom more quickly. But where the bulbs are stimulated into growth before the roots have formed, stunting will result, and in some cases it may cause the bulbs to be quite 'blind'.

In no circumstances should the bulbs be placed in a room where there is heat in any form until they have had two months for forming their roots under quite cool conditions. Place them in a cellar, garage or outhouse; or, where provided with drainage holes, there is nowhere better than in a bed of ashes exposed to the elements. Lack of light and completely cool conditions are essential factors in the first eight weeks of all newly-planted bulbs to be flowered indoors; and with most of the miniature bulbs, such as the Daffodils, Snowdrops, Irises and Chionodoxas, there is preference for cool conditions throughout. The secret of success with all bulbs to be brought into bloom indoors is to allow them plenty of time to form their roots and to develop. Introduce them to the light as slowly as possible and keep the compost neither too dry nor too moist. Extremes, both of temperature and of compost conditions, are to be avoided.

Specially prepared fibre, which is generally mixed with oyster shell and charcoal to maintain sweetness where containers are without drainage holes, is the usual medium for indoor rooting. Bulb fibre is composed mainly of dry peat or coconut fibre which will require a considerable amount of moisture to make it damp and friable before the bulbs are planted. Never plant into dry bulb fibre, for it is quite impossible to add the necessary moisture afterwards; and this is where so many go wrong. To give that little extra 'body' to the compost, so that moisture requirements may be better controlled, try to mix in a small quantity of pasture loam; a bucketful brought home in the boot of the car is sufficient for a dozen pots or bowls when mixed with the fibre. While forming roots, the bulbs will require little moisture in such a compost, but more should be given as soon as growth commences. And be sure to keep them cool.

After flowering, the bowls should be placed in a shady corner outdoors, perhaps beneath the greenhouse bench or in a cellar or garage, so that the foliage may be dried off and the bulbs may be stored until required again; or they may be divided and replanted in the open ground as soon as they have finished flowering.

30. *Narcissus.* 'W. P. Milner'

31. *Scilla sibirica*. 'Spring Beauty'

32. *Scilla Tubergeniana*, whose delicate silver-blue flowers make an attractive subject in the rock garden

33. *Narcissus cyclamineus.* Hybrid 'February Gold'

CHAPTER 11

Half-hardy Bulbs for the Cool Greenhouse

*Advantage of indoor bulbs—Housing the bulbs—Planting and care of
the bulbs—Half-hardy bulbs for a cold greenhouse—Hardy bulbs for
the alpine house—Forcing bulbs*

Advantages of indoor bulbs

The most inexpensive structure may be used to provide protection for a wide variety of half-hardy bulbs which, in a northerly garden, could not be relied upon to bloom to perfection unprotected. In addition, miniature bulbs which are suitable for a rockery, or trough garden, may also be grown under cover so that the flowers may be enjoyed several weeks before they would come into bloom outdoors. Given protection of some sort the bulbs will reveal a clearness of colour, due to their blooms opening quite clean, which they were never known to possess. No heat will be required apart from the natural warmth of the sun's rays for the miniature bulbs will, with but one or two exceptions, be quite intolerant of forcing conditions. Even bulbs of South African origin will give a better account of themselves where grown in a cool house, for all they require is protection from excessive winter miosture, for the bulbs and protection from cold winds for the blooms in spring. Bulbs given protection will come into bloom fully a month earlier than those growing in the open ground, and the blooms, free from deposits of soot and sulphur and from soil particles, will take on a luminous beauty. Those which bloom outdoors during late autumn and winter in a town garden will frequently be grimy, especially during foggy weather, while heavy rains at this time of the year may 'dash' the blooms when at their peak of perfection. Flowers which are attractive to birds will also benefit from protection, and mice will rarely attack bulbs or corms growing under glass, as they will sometimes do when these are in the open ground.

A cold frame, deeply constructed of secondhand bricks or breeze blocks to allow stems of anything up to twelve inches in length ample room, will prove quite suitable for those half-hardy bulbs which may be taken indoors when coming into bloom. A cold house structure, in which the bulbs may be grown and flowered on benches, will be useful, for here other winter- and spring-flowering plants may be grown, such as the Show auriculas which require protection for the flowers if they are to be seen at their best. In this way, the most inexpensive structure may be made to yield its full quota of beauty at a time when the garden may be covered with frost and snow. It may be erected even where there is no garden, perhaps on a veranda where it may also serve as a sun room; or in a small courtyard where tubs or troughs may be the only alternative means of exhibiting one's plants. The bulbs may spend the whole of their life in such a structure for they may be started into growth beneath the benches in pots or pans covered with ashes, until they have built up a strong rooting system. They may then be gradually introduced to the light by placing them on the benches. Where no heat is available, the half-hardy bulbs should not be placed on the benches until the spring sun gathers strength, or they may suffer damage if severe frost prevails at night. The most hardy bulbs, such as the Crocuses, Snowdrops, Chionodoxas and Iris species, all delightful subjects for pot culture, may be set on the benches just as soon as they have become well rooted, though where growing throughout under quite cold conditions there is not so great a necessity for the bulbs to build up a strong root system. In a cold greenhouse, the bulbs will continue to form roots even when exposed to full light, though the more roots they form the better will they bloom.

Housing the bulbs

A very simple structure may be erected from stout timber (for the upright supports) with tongue and grooved weather boarding to enclose the lower part of the structure to a height of three feet from the ground. It may be built over a hard surface or one of soil covered with ashes and made quite firm. The upper portion of the structure need not be of glass, which would add to the expense, but may be enclosed with polythene sheeting or Windolite, both of which will prove extremely durable and will admit the essential light and exclude unpleasant weather. The roof should have a slope of about one foot from the back to the front so as to allow both snow and rainwater to drain away as quickly as possible. The roofing material should be Windolite, made secure by nailing it to numerous cross bars which will prevent the roof from collapsing under the weight of heavy snow. Nothing elaborate is called for, just something weatherproof. The door, probably obtainable for a few shillings from an old government property auction, may be fixed to the back of the structure. The benches should be erected by fixing the woodwork at the top of the weather boarding. They must be quite secure, for when filled with pots their weight will be considerable. Flat iron sheeting should be used to cover the benches and this should be covered to a depth of one inch with washed gravel on which the pots will stand. The ground beneath the benches should be covered with ashes, for here the pots will be placed while the bulbs are forming their roots; and again after flowering, while they die back. Bulbs to be grown in the house may also be placed under the bench both before and after flowering or they may, of course, be placed beneath a bed of ashes outdoors while they form roots. Winter- and spring-flowering bulbs will also fit in with a cold-house tomato crop, the tomato plants being set out in pots or boxes on the benches early in May and trained over the roof of the house. Or summer-flowering annuals, such as the new Hybrid petunias, may be grown in pots, the plants being obtained in the seedling stage after having been hardened.

Where bulbs are placed beneath the benches to form roots, canvas or sacking should be fixed to the front of the benches to exclude as much light as possible; and where bulbs are being grown in a frame, the lights, which may be made either of Windolite or glass, should also be covered while rooting is taking place. The same canvas may also be used to protect the plants from the midday sun during April and May when in full bloom, for this will enable the blooms to remain fresh for a considerably longer time. A lean-to 'glasshouse' may be constructed even more reasonably and for bulbs, Auriculas and most other winter- and spring-flowering plants, a northerly situation will prove quite suitable.

Planting and care of the bulbs

Bulbs to be grown in a cold greenhouse should be grown either in pots or pans which will be complete with a drainage hole. Pans made of earthenware and about six inches deep will provide a more generous display, for a dozen small bulbs may be planted in each pan.

Where the bulbs bear their bloom on stems almost twelve inches tall they should be supported by placing thin sticks or canes around the sides of the pots to which green twine is fastened so as to prevent the foliage and bloom from becoming untidy; or twigs may be inserted among the foliage. Coloured bulb bowls should not be used for cold-house culture for they will often be without drainage holes, and bulbs planted in such containers will rarely prove successful.

The pots or pans should be well crocked before adding the compost which should be of 2 parts friable turf loam, 1 part peat, leaf mould or old mushroom bed compost and 1 part coarse sand or grit, to which should be added a sprinkling of bone meal and some lime rubble where suitable. Do not obtain soil from the garden, for where situated in or near a town this may be in an inert condition through constant lack of attention, or may be of an acid nature through continual deposits of soot and sulphur. Garden soil will also contain numerous weed seeds which will germinate and prove troublesome when the bulbs are coming into bloom. Fresh, friable loam from pasture land will prove ideal for all bulbs, and the compost should be thoroughly mixed together and stored under cover until ready for use.

To plant the bulbs, first place the compost in the pans to the necessary depth, which will be about two-thirds of the depth of the container. Into the compost the bulbs are pressed with the broader and more rounded end downwards, as this is the rooting end. Space out the bulbs evenly, allowing about two inches between each or about half that distance where the bulbs are very small. They should then be carefully covered with the compost to a depth of half an inch or slightly more and so that the surface of the compost is just below the rim of the pan. The label bearing the name of the species or variety should be inserted at the side of the pot, which will then be ready for covering to exclude light so that the bulbs will not come prematurely into growth. Certain bulbs will, however, not require a period in darkness.

Those which do need a period of darkness should then be placed either beneath the benches or in a sheltered corner in the open, where they should be covered with ashes or sand to a depth of six inches. If placed beneath the greenhouse benches the bulbs should first be given a thorough watering which may be sufficient to keep the compost moist until the pots are lifted on to the benches when they are brought into bloom. The bulbs will be kept in the dark either by covering with ashes or by hanging canvas around the benches. Those which are to bloom during autumn and early winter should be potted early in August, and so that they are kept as cool as possible until forming their roots, they are best placed in a dark corner outdoors until removed to the greenhouse at the end of September. Those which will bloom during the latter weeks of winter and during early spring should be potted in early October and may be brought into the light towards the end of November. Many of the half-hardy bulbs are best potted late in October and will be placed on the benches while rooting. They should be watered sparingly during the winter months.

Those which are to be brought into bloom indoors, after a period in total darkness, should be introduced to the light by decrees, first removing the canvas where they bulbs are being rooted beneath the benches. Where they have been grown outdoors beneath ashes, when first introduced to the house they should be placed under the benches for several days without the canvas being fixed to the sides. After about a week the pots may be placed on the benches in full light.

There will be need for little ventilation during the winter months; in fact, plants growing in a cold house will require none at all; but as the sun gathers strength, more fresh air should be admitted either by leaving the door open or by opening the ventilators of a properly constructed greenhouse. During periods of strong sunlight brown paper should be tacked on to the inside of the structure to provide shading, or canvas may be used on the sunny side where necessary.

Little moisture will be required by the growing bulbs during autumn and winter, for after a thorough watering at planting time they will usually obtain all the moisture necessary from the atmosphere. As conditions become warmer, the compost should be watered whenever it begins to dry out, and on all sunny days both foliage and blooms will benefit from spraying with clean water around midday.

After flowering, the pots should be placed on their sides beneath the benches and all water should be withheld. When the foliage has died down it may be removed with care and at the same time the bulbs should be shaken from the pots, cleaned of all soil and stored in boxes of dry peat until ready for potting again.

Half-hardy bulbs for a cold greenhouse

ANOMATHECA. This is a charming little plant which seems sufficiently hardy for growing outdoors where it can be given a sheltered, sunny position, but only in small pots in the cold greenhouse will it be fully appreciated. It is most valuable in that it blooms during the latter weeks of summer when there will be few other bulbs in bloom.

The corms should be planted in March whether growing outdoors or in pots. Four corms should be planted to a 60-size pot and they should not be removed after flowering for they will increase rapidly and soon fill the pot, sending up numerous six-inch stems at the end of which appear several tiny salmon-red flowers blotched with crimson. *A. juncea* is rarer and bears its rose-pink blooms on nine- to ten-inch stems. Where planting outdoors in a more exposed garden it is better to lift the bulbs in October and store in dry peat until planted out again in March.

BABIANA. This lovely flowering plant should be given the same treatment as the *Tritonia* and *Streptanthera*, the bulbs being planted in 60-size pots in November and kept almost dry until they start into growth in early spring. The pots should be placed on the benches or in a frame but not be kept in the dark. The bulbs will bloom in early summer and after flowering should not be emptied from the pots but should be dried off with care and retained in the pots until ready for starting into growth again in the New Year, when they should be topped up with fresh loam.

The Babianas are most inexpensive, one of the most attractive being *B. disticha*, which bears eight-inch spikes of pale blue during May and June; and *B. plicata* has rich violet flowers on six-inch stems. Most distinct and beautiful is *B. rubro-cyanea*, the deep blue flowers on three-inch stems having a crimson eye. Another most striking variety is *B. Bainesii*, a new introduction from the Orange Free State which bears its slender tubes of brilliant violet during July.

BEGONIA. The colourful 'Multiflora' begonias make excellent subjects for cold-house culture, planted one to a 60-size pot. The tubers should be started into growth in April in boxes of peat as described in Chapter 5, and when the first leaf appears they should be lifted with care and transferred to the pots. All that they require is a peaty compost which is kept moist, and this may mean copious amounts of water during the mid-summer months, while the plants in bloom will benefit from a daily syringeing with clean water. A weekly application of dilute manure water will prolong the flowering period and build up a sturdy corm for next year's flowering. After flowering, the plants should be allowed to die back gradually, when the tubers should be shaken from the pots, cleaned and stored in dry peat.

BRODIAEA. These early summer-flowering bulbous plants from California should be grown in a cold house where their beauty may be appreciated to the full; though, being almost hardy, they may be grown outdoors in all but the most exposed situations. The 'Californian Fire Cracker', with its pendant flowers of brilliant red tipped with green, is quite outstanding for indoor culture and should be planted in November. The bulbs are brought on in the usual way to bloom in June. There are several worthwhile species which have been described previously.

CALOCHORTUS. In the open this is a difficult plant to grow for it likes a sunny position to ripen its bulbs, a well-drained, sandy soil, and protection in winter. In other words, it is best grown indoors. The dwarf forms are known as 'Star' or 'Butterfly' Tulips for it has tulip-like leaves, and the blooms open like butterflies in flight. As William Robinson wrote, 'They form one of the most charming groups of hardy bulbous plants,' but they are hardy only where everything is in their favour. By planting different species in a favourable position outdoors, or in pots or pans in the alpine house, flowers may be enjoyed from the end of April, when the lovely *C. Benthamii* comes into bloom, until well into July. *C. Benthamii* is perhaps the easiest to grow and bears lemon-yellow blooms covered with silk-like hairs, on strong six-inch stems. Then follow *C. amoenus*, having rose-pink flowers on eight-inch stems, and *C. albus* with waxy-white, hair-covered flowers in profusion. If they are to flower indoors, bulbs should be planted in November, and care must be taken not to give them too much water during winter.

HAEMANTHUS. Known as the 'Red Cape Lily', this plant, though dwarf, grows from a large bulb and is quite magnificent. Though generally grown in a warm greenhouse, it is late summer- and early autumn-flowering, and so may be grown in the alpine house. The bulbs should be potted singly in early April and should be kept as cool as possible until they have formed their roots. Afterwards they should be brought into growth by providing them with more moisture, and as the sun gathers strength the plants will require quite heavy waterings. The moisture must be gradually withheld as the bulbs are dried off under the bench in autumn. They will require re-potting only in alternate years. *H. coccineus* bears umbels of brilliant crimson-red blooms from blood-red footstalks which are held on stems nine to ten inches in length. There are other handsome forms which are rather too tall to come within the scope of this book.

HOMERIA. This is an unusual-looking bulbous plant from the Cape and may be better known by the name of *Bobartia aurantiaca*. *Homeria collina* bears orange-yellow or orange-pink flowers on twelve-inch stems and like the *Tritonia* and *Strepthanthera* it should not be forced or grown in the dark, otherwise its foliage and flower stems will be weak and untidy. Only one narrow leaf comes from a single bulb and from the fold appears a spray of starry flowers more than two inches across and attractively blotched with purple. Under glass the flowers appear during May.

RHODOHYPOXIS. The species *R. Baurii*, a native of South Africa, is a charming little plant bearing rosy-red star-like flowers on only three-inch stems during early summer. It likes a gritty, well-drained soil but should never lack moisture when in bloom. The bulbs appear quite hardy where planted in a pocket on the rockery, and where the garden is sheltered, but the plants may be most appreciated in pans in the alpine house.

ROMULEA. For growing in pans in the alpine house there is no more rewarding plant, nor one which will remain longer in bloom. Bulbs planted in early October will come into bloom early in May and will remain colourful until midsummer. From amidst short bristle-like foliage appear the funnel-shaped flowers, those of *R. sabulosa* being of bright cherry-red and those of *R. columnae* greenish-white, veined with purple. A rather more tender form, *R. macowanii*, has flowers of bright golden-yellow. The bulbs should be treated like any other ordinary bulb but should be kept on the dry side throughout.

SPARAXIS. Like most of the South African bulbous plants, the 'Harlequin Flower', *Sparaxis tricolor*, is spectacular. It is so called on account of the brilliant colours of the blooms which vary from cream to mauve, cerise and scarlet, colourings being accentuated by their dark centres which are revealed when the blooms open. The flowers are similar in appearance to freesias and being of a like hardiness the plants should be given the same treatment as that recommended for *Tritonia* and *Streptanthera* and described under these plants. Under cover, the plants bloom during May, the flowers being borne on nine- to ten-inch stems. The bulbs hate disturbance and should not be shaken from the pots for several years.

STREPTANTHERA. This is one of the most striking of all the South African bulbous plants, the blooms of *S. cuprea coccinea* being of a unique shade of coppery scarlet with a jet black centre. They are borne on stems six to eight inches long. Bulbs may be obtained for a shilling each and four or five should be planted to a pan. Indoors, the bulbs will bloom in April and early May and six weeks later in a favourable position outdoors, but it is not advisable to plant the bulbs outside in the North.

This plant should be given much the same culture as for freesias; that is, they should not be kept in the dark but should be kept as dry as possible during winter while rooting is taking place in a cool greenhouse or frame. After flowering, no foliage should be removed until it has died back completely, for as long as it remains even partially green it will continue to supply the bulbs with food for next season. Do not remove the bulbs from the pots or pans, keep the compost dry during the resting period, then top up with fresh compost and bring the bulbs into growth again in the New Year.

TECOPHILAEA. This is one of the most interesting and beautiful of all bulbous plants and is known as the 'Chilean Blue Crocus'. It should not be grown outdoors, for it blooms in March and there is no time to lift and replant each year. An exception may be made in a sheltered valley in South Devon or Cornwall. For the cold greenhouse, however, no plant is finer. *T. cyanocrocus* bears starry crocuslike flowers of a glorious shade of gentian blue on three-inch stems, while the species *T. Leichtlinii* has sky-blue flowers with a white throat. Indoors they bloom in early spring, the blooms being enhanced by the short glossy green leaves. Both forms are deliciously fragrant.

The bulbs are best grown in pans in a compost composed of equal parts of loam, sand and leaf mould (or peat) and they should be kept under the benches until the New Year so that hard frost will cause them no harm.

TRITONIA. *T. crocata*, which may be grown outside with protection, is a most beautiful plant for a cold greenhouse. It should be treated like the *Streptanthera*, the bulbs being planted in pots about mid-November and grown on the greenhouse bench, keeping the compost on the dry side until rooting has taken place. When the bulbs are coming into growth in early spring, more water should be given; but as the foliage dies back moisture should be gradually reduced. After flowering, the bulbs should be treated in the same way as the *Streptanthera*. *T. crocata* bears its glowing salmon-orange flowers on ten-inch stems above handsome, glossy, strap-like foliage, and *T. Lyalina* bears flowers of a soft shade of salmon-pink. A few twigs should be used to support the blooms as they begin to open.

Hardy bulbs for the alpine house

All the hardy miniature flowering bulbs may also be grown in the alpine house where they are particularly attractive growing in pans in which the compost should be covered with small chippings to prevent splashing of the blooms. Among the most suitable of the hardy bulbs are the Cyclamens, *Erythronium dens-canis*, *Muscari azureum* and *botryoides*, *Chionodoxa luciliae*, Winter Aconites, most of the Crocus species, *Fritillaria pudica*, *Galanthus Elwesii*, *Iris Danfordiae* and *I. reticulata*, most of the Tulip species of compact habit, and the Miniature daffodils.

The tiny Narcissus species make delightful plants either in small pots or in pans where they may remain for several seasons and if left undisturbed, they will flower freely for long periods. For growing in the warm atmosphere of a room the large-flowered Daffodils should be used, and those miniature hybrids which are more free flowering than the species themselves and which may take twelve months to become established.

The 'Hoop Petticoat' daffodils, the 'Rush-leaved' daffodil and the 'Polyanthus' narcissus as well as the tiny *N. minimus* and *N. minor* are charming subjects for pans and will come into bloom at the beginning of March. To prolong the season, plant *N. tenuior*, the 'Silver Jonquil', and *N. Watieri* from Morocco. The same bulbs growing outdoors will not come into bloom until those grown under cover are coming to an end. All these bulbs should be kept in the dark for six weeks after being planted in the pots and before being placed on the greenhouse benches. After flowering they should be dried off beneath the benches.

It is not generally realized that both the Anemone and the Oxalis species make beautiful cold-house plants. Here they will attain a greater perfection than in the often wind-swept garden. They will not, of course, withstand any degree of forcing, neither are they suitable for growing in the diffused light of a living-room, for here the stems would grow tall and weak and the blooms would be devoid of colour; but as pot plants in the alpine house they are most attractive. Outstanding is *Anemone blanda*, and if the corms are planted in June around the sides of a 48-pot, they will produce their brilliant blue flowers throughout winter and early spring. *A. apennina* may also be grown in this way, and *A. fulgens* and the 'Poppy' Anemones may be grown in deep boxes for their cut bloom, which will be produced when deep snow may cover those same plants growing outdoors.

Of the Wood Sorrels suitable for an alpine house, *Oxalis variabilis* from South Africa is particularly pleasing. In fact, it is at its loveliest then, for its large clear pink flowers are borne on three-inch stems during late autumn. The Wood Sorrels bloom the whole year round in the alpine house, starting with *O. cernua* with its drooping yellow flowers which first appear in February and continue until May when *O. braziliensis* shows its flowers of wine-red on three-inch stems. Plant with it *O. adenophylla* from Chile, which has rich grey foliage and cream and pink flowers. They will be in bloom until August when *O. lobata* starts into growth, to bear its flowers of burnished gold until *O. variabilis* takes over and will continue to bear its pink flowers until February, thus giving complete continuity. These bulbous plants should not be started into growth in shade but should be kept as cool as possible both while rooting and during the rest periods, which vary greatly as to time of year.

Forcing bulbs

There are a number of bulbs which will withstand quite warm conditions either in a heated greenhouse or in the home. The tiny 'Duc van Thol' tulips are obtainable in scarlet, white and yellow and are grown under specialized forcing conditions by the million by nursery growers to supply the Christmas and New Year market, the plants being transferred when in bud and bloom from the forcing boxes to fancy bowls. It is possibly because these charming plants are so frequently presented in this way that enthusiasts have come to believe that all bulbs will prove more successful where grown throughout in a fancy bowl. I can only repeat that very much better results will be obtained by using an earthenware container provided with ample drainage holes.

The early flowering Hyacinths 'Rosalie' and 'Vanguard' will also stand up to hard forcing to flower in the early New Year, while a number of the dwarf early single Tulips, which grow about nine inches tall, may be brought into bloom during the latter days of March. Amongst the most suitable are 'Proserpine', silky carmine-pink; 'Joffre', deep golden yellow; and the scarlet-flowering 'Brilliant Star'. Both the Duc van Thol tulips and the early hyacinths will often have been 'prepared' so that they will come quickly into bloom when subjected to heat. To achieve this condition, they will have been kept in cold storage, and should be planted almost immediately they are received. But this does not mean they may be taken into heat at once. It is even more important that the bulbs should be allowed fully eight weeks in which to form the strong rooting system which is vital if they are to be subjected to high temperatures. The Duc van Thols should be planted in boxes or pots about October 1st, together with the other early Tulips and Hyacinths; and after eight weeks under cool, dark, conditions, they may be introduced to a warm greenhouse or warm room, and will be happy in a temperature of up to 60° F. In such a temperature the bulbs will come into bloom by the end of December, but in ordinary warm room temperatures, not until late in January. The Hyacinths and the other early Tulips will not bloom until March and should not be taken indoors until mid-December.

For forcing, top-quality bulbs will be required and they will not be of use for forcing again, though they may still be planted in the garden. Deep earthenware bowls or pans are the most suitable containers and five or six 12-cm. size bulbs may be planted in each. The bulbs should be handled carefully as Tulips bruise easily. When planted, the top of the bulbs should be just covered with the compost. Water thoroughly and place the bulbs beneath ashes either outside or in a cellar or garage where they should require no further watering until taken into a warm temperature. The cooler the bulbs are kept whilst rooting, the more rapidly will they respond to warmth; but do not subject them to sudden changes of temperature. When ready for forcing, the bulbs should first be given a temperature of about 45° F., and this should be increased gradually until a limit of 60° F. may possibly be achieved. As the bulbs make growth they will require copious amounts of water under these conditions, and if lacking moisture at any time flowering will be delayed and stunted growth may result.

As the plants come into bloom, they may need some support, for the stems will not be so sturdy as where 'grown cool'. Wire supports, procurable from any sundriesman, should be used, and will be almost invisible. As soon as the plants come into bloom they should be given reduced temperatures so as to prolong the flowering season as much as possible, though fluctuations of temperature should be avoided and draughts eliminated, otherwise the stems may collapse.

124

Part Two

MINIATURE BULBS

A description of species and varieties

Miniature Bulbs: Alphabetical List

ALLIUM

These are the 'Ornamental Onions' or 'Flowering Garlics', excellent for massing in the shrubbery, especially where the soil is dry and sandy. They are most colourful and not only are they extremely hardy but they bloom during May and June when most other bulbs will be coming to an end. The tiny star-shaped flowers are massed together, in the case of several to form ball-like heads like those of *Primula denticulata*. To Parkinson, they were 'Mollies' and he mentions that 'the flowers do abide a great while blown (open) before they fade'.

The alliums prefer a sunny position so that the bulbs are able to ripen fully. In this way, they will increase rapidly and be free-flowering. They are ideal plants for the labour-saving garden in that they may be left untouched for several years before it is necessary to lift and divide them.

The end of October is the most suitable time to plant, setting them three inches deep; and if the soil is heavy, sprinkling a little sand around the bulbs. Though many are tall, there are a number of dwarf species which will come within the scope of this book to give colour from May until September. The plants are native of Central Asia and Eastern Europe, *A. moly* being introduced to England in 1604. They are extremely hardy.

Species

A. anceps. A very tiny species bearing, during August, rich pink flowers on six-inch stems. This is a valuable late-summer plant for the alpine garden.

A. cyaneum. A native of China and valuable in that it blooms during July and August. It is the smallest of all, growing only four inches tall, and is most suitable for the scree. Above its grass-like leaves, on wiry stems, hang clusters of brilliant pale blue flowers which are enhanced by their bright green centre.

A. karataviense. From Afghanistan, it produces its globular heads

127

of purple-grey throughout May, but its chief claim to inclusion in the shrubbery lies in its beautiful grey, or crimson-tinted, foliage made even more beautiful by a spangling of dew. 10–12 inches.

A. moly. The best species for naturalising in grass or the shrubbery, for it increases rapidly, rather too quickly perhaps, and so should not be planted too near other choice bulbs. Called the 'Golden Garlic', its bright yellow flowers are borne in umbels during June, and are excellent for cutting. 12 inches.

A. ostrowskianum. Probably the best of all the alliums for it produces its compact heads of bright lilac-pink, rather like those of *Primula denticulata*, during May and June on six-inch stems. It should be planted as an edging to a border or path.

ANEMONE

Besides the 'Poppy' Anemones which are most valuable plants for summer bedding, the Anemone species may be used in numerous ways about the garden; and nowhere are they more at home than where planted in drifts in the shrubbery, where they may be left for years undisturbed. *A. nemorosa*, the Wood Anemone, may also be planted beneath mature trees, for it likes shade and a continually moist soil.

All the Anemones, with the possible exception of *A. nemorosa*, like a soil containing some lime; they are never happy in an acid soil, and the shrubbery of a town garden should be dressed with hydrated lime before the tubers are planted. And do not plant too closely together. Six inches should be allowed between tubers, for they form a vigorous rooting system and will quickly exhaust the soil if planted too close.

To see them at their best plant in drifts, but keep the colours separate. For example, near a drift of *A. blanda atro-coerulea*, with its dainty gentian-blue flowers, plant the new rosy-red variety, 'Charmer' and they will soon form a patterned carpet. Seed may be sown where the plants are to bloom and it will detract little from their beauty if they do not come true to colour.

Species

A. apennina. Producing blooms of clearest blue during March and April, this is a most useful species in that it is extremely hardy and will bloom to perfection in a shaded position. It should be massed

34. *Narcissus canaliculatus.* A miniature, Polyanthus Narcissus having two to four flowers on each stem. The perianth is white and reflexed, the cup golden. It has a sweet scent. Height six inches. Flowering in April

36. *Muscari,* 'Blue Pearl'

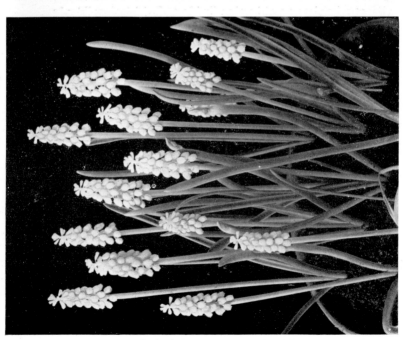

35. *Muscari botryoides album*

37a. Miniature bulbs set out in six-inch pans two-thirds filled with compost. The pans are then filled up with more compost and the surface made firm

37b. 'Plunging' in a backyard using a simple wooden frame. The pans of bulbs are placed on a layer of sand to ensure drainage and are then surrounded and covered over with peat

38*a*. 'Plunging' (1). Pots of bulbs placed in a trench prior to covering with soil. The pots are sunk to the rim and should stand on a layer of sand or ashes to ensure drainage

38*b*. 'Plunging' (2). A six-inch layer of soil is placed over the pots in the trench. Section shows how pots are completely surrounded and protected —note layer of sand for drainage

under trees or in the shrubbery, where it may be left undisturbed. The pale green fern-like foliage adds to its attraction. It is a great lover of lime. It may be increased by dividing the roots in autumn. 6 inches.

A. blanda. This is the 'Grecian Windflower' which prefers a position of full sun when it will come into bloom with the first warm rays of the early spring sunshine. With their short stems, these should be planted around ornamental trees or to the front of a shrubbery, their prettily cut foliage being almost as lovely as the blooms. As with all the Anemone species, planting should be done in September to allow the tubers plenty of time to become established before the frosts. *A. blanda atro-coerulea* bears masses of deep blue flowers, *rosea* bears blooms of a delicate rose-pink colour. The new variety, 'Charmer', is a great improvement on *rosea*, the blooms being larger and of a deep rosy-red colour. The new variety, 'White Splendour', should be planted among those of rich colouring. It has huge snowy-white flowers which remain in condition for a very long time.

As *A. blanda* soon loses its foliage after flowering, it may be planted on a bank or in grass which is kept short by cutting with a sickle or with shears, the first cut being given during June. The plants may be increased by division of the roots immediately after flowering and before the foliage dies back. 3 inches.

A. fulgens. This is the 'Scarlet Windflower' of the French Riviera and the Pyrenees, a superb sight when planted in masses, or it may be grown under cloches or in open beds both for cutting and for garden decoration, the rich scarlet star-like blooms being carried on twelve-inch stems. It likes a dry, sandy soil and a position of full sun, and for this reason it makes a superb show in East Anglian gardens and in Kent and Sussex, though not seen nearly so often as it should be. There is a semi-double form which sets no seed known as *A. Pavonina*, from which the 'St. Bavo' strain is descended, and which is occasionally grown as a commercial flower.

Extremely tolerant of frost as it is, but in no way happy when growing in a moist, humus-laden soil, it is essential to incorporate plenty of sand or grit in the soil before planting. As it does not come perfectly true from seed, propagation is by division of the roots which is best done when they are dormant in easly autumn, also the best time to plant the tubers. If the plants are to be covered with cloches for winter flowering, plant six inches apart in rows four inches wide, and cover with cloches in November. The starry, narrow-petalled flowers are carried on twelve-inch stems, the cut bloom remaining fresh in water for up to ten days. Naturally in bloom during early summer, this is a splendid plant for a sunny shrubbery, or even to provide colour in the herbaceous border, the plants being set in clumps of six or seven. It persists well from year to year.

A. nemorosa. This, our native Wood Anemone, is extremely free flowering and bears a single white bloom, attractively tinted with pink on the exterior. Even more showy is the variety 'Royal Blue', with a very large bloom of rich lavender; *Robinsoniana* has a neat bloom of an exquisite shade of silvery lavender with yellow anthers. Of this form, the Rev. Harpur Crewe said, 'All fade before its simple and innocent loveliness.' This is the plant which William Robinson found, quite by accident, growing at the foot of a wall in the Oxford Botanical Gardens. *A. nemorosa* prefers a shady position and a cool, moist soil. The plants continue to bloom until June. 6 inches.

A. palmata. It is quite hardy but must be given a deep root run and a soil capable of holding summer moisture. It is the 'Cyclamen-leaf' anemone, with large glossy leaves and cup-shaped blooms of pale yellow, with deep yellow anthers. It blooms during May and June when most of the other species have finished flowering, and is a most arresting sight with its foliage and flowers gleaming in the sunlight. When once established, the plants should be left almost indefinitely without disturbance. 8 inches. There is a white form, *alba.*

A. ranunculoides. This is a valuable rock garden plant for it is of dainty, compact habit. It bears its deep golden-yellow blooms amid attractive dark bronzy foliage during spring and remains long in bloom. The best form is *superba*, which bears darker bronzy foliage and a more refined bloom. It grows equally as well in shade and in full sun and, like all anemones, prefers a soil containing plenty of peat or leaf mould and of course some lime. That great authority on alpine plants, Mr. T. C. Mansfield, suggests planting this anemone among the dwarf lime-loving heathers which will provide that protection from cold spring winds which the plants enjoy. It may be increased by root division in autumn but should be disturbed as little as possible.

ANOMATHECA. See Chapter 11.

ANTHERICUM LILIASTRUM

This is 'St. Bruno's Lily', which blooms in June and early July. It enjoys partial shade and a well-drained soil and is a quite delightful plant. Its white trumpets are borne on twelve-inch stems from a mass of grass-like foliage, the blooms, when cut, lasting long in water. It is to be found growing naturally in the alpine meadows of Central Europe so it is quite at home in the wild garden, several bulbs planted together making a charming display, the blooms like miniature Madonna lilies.

BABIANA. See Chapter 11.

BEGONIA. See Chapter 11.

BRODIAEA

Known as 'Californian Hyacinths', the Brodiaeas are exquisite little plants, in flower from the end of May until mid-July. The sturdy stems carry at their tops up to half a dozen gentian-like flowers. They are not quite completely hardy, and so should be given a mulch in early December. Over the clumps should be placed a quantity of weathered ash. There are, however, exceptions to the rule of hardiness. *Brodiaea coccinea* is perfectly able to withstand a severe winter in a well-drained soil, and *B. uniflora*, the *Tritelia* of our gardens, is completely hardy. All of them may be grown outdoors unprotected in the south and West Country, where I have grown them to perfection in a sandy, well-drained soil; but for the more northerly garden they should be given winter protection except for the two species mentioned.

Planting

Being natives of California, these must be given a sunny position and a soil which will warm up quickly in early summer. To achieve this, plenty of sand, shingle and leaf mould should be well worked into the soil before planting takes place in September. Some thoroughly rotted manure is helpful, too, for these are plants which should not be disturbed once planted. I find that a mixture of dry poultry manure, peat and some strawy farmyard manure, thoroughly mixed, to which some loam and coarse sand have been added, will prove ideal if allowed to remain in a heap for two months before being added to the soil.

Where the bulbs are being grown in grass or in the shrub border, the same compost should be placed into each square foot of ground where the bulbs are to be set. But first see that the ground is clear of all perennial weeds. Then plant them four inches deep, placing some sand around each bulb when in position. They should be planted four inches apart and in groups of four bulbs. Several species are ideal for the rockery and are at their best when planted round stones, placing a large proportion of shingle around and above the bulbs for winter protection. They are quite at home in the shrubbery, where the bulbs can receive some sunshine to ripen them; they are in their element at the base of a wall facing south. See also Chapter 10.

Species

B. coccinea. Known as the 'Californian Firecracker', this is one of the most outstanding of all garden plants. The brilliant red blooms are attractively tipped with green, making a most striking display throughout June and July. The flowers are carried on twelve-inch stems, but may grow rather taller.

    B. congesta. It is native of the North-west Coast of America and bears small spikes of lilac-blue on twelve-inch stems during June.

    B. crocea. This is a variety well suited to the alpine garden for the dainty yellow flowers are borne profusely on six-inch stems during May and early June.

    B. grandiflora. Dwarf of habit and of an enchanting sky-blue colour, this species produces its bloom abundantly throughout June. 6–8 inches.

    B. ixioides splendens. This is a rare and beautiful form from California, with umbels of pale yellow flowers during June. 9 inches.

    B. minor. A native of America, it is known as the 'Missouri Hyacinth'. A charming little plant, it grows only six inches tall and bears, during June, umbels of deepest blue.

    B. multiflora. Quite easy to establish, it bears compact umbels of rich lavender-coloured flowers during mid-summer. 9 inches.

BULBOCODIUM

This lovely spring-flowering plant is generally mistaken for a Crocus. Some believe that it is a spring-flowering species of the Colchicum, as it comes into bloom before producing its leaves. It has another similarity in that it is called the 'spring' Meadow saffron.

It really appears to be a Colchicum that is flowering at the wrong time, though on closer inspection it may be seen that its segments are held together only by the soil, the familiar long tube of both the crocus and colchicum being absent. The plant is most valuable for early March flowering in almost any position in the garden. It is little troubled by soil conditions though it flourishes to perfection in one that is well drained, and it should be planted where it is able to receive its share of the early spring sunshine. It is not such a lover of the cool, shady places as the Dog's Tooth Violet and seems to be at its best on a rockery, or planted in drifts beneath a wall facing the sun. The bulbs should be planted between September and early November, about three inches deep.

Species

B. vernum. This is the only species known to the author and is quite outstanding, producing its lavender-pink flowers, shaded with red, throughout March. When open the blooms are star-like, which adds to their charm, though as they grow older the segments (petals) fall apart and they become somewhat untidy. The flowers grow about three inches above soil level.

CALOCHORTUS. See Chapter 10.

CHIONODOXA

'Glory of the Snow' is its more popular name, and very suitable it is too, but as with so many of the small flowering bulbs, we tend to plant but one or two species and neglect the others which are even choicer and are just as inexpensive and easy to obtain. The American, Mrs. Louise Wilder, in *Adventures in My Garden*, describes them perfectly as being 'like exquisite bits of enamel-work'.

They will increase more rapidly than any other flowering bulb and will remain in bloom throughout March and April. Their native haunt is Greece and Turkey, and the name means literally 'Glory of the Snow'. It is a relatively new plant, introduced in 1877 by Mr. George Maw who discovered a bank of it 5,000 feet above sea-level. The bulbs first flowered in this country the following year.

The Chionodoxa is a valuable little flower as it does not appear to resent the frequent cold winds and sleet showers of early spring. Unlike the Crocus it refuses to close up its flowers as if protecting itself from the elements, although the vivid blue, pink and white blooms look deceptively delicate. Planted in pots and allowed to bloom in a frame or cold house in March, they make a welcome addition to the spring display.

Planting

Ideal plants for the alpine garden or for the front of a border or shrubbery, where they may receive their fair share of sunshine, the Chionodoxas should be planted in September as freely as possible. Plant in clusters, setting the bulbs no more than two inches deep. The plant is not so tolerant of damp, shady conditions as the Snowdrop or Winter aconite, so reserve the more shady corners for other flowers. The Chionodoxa enjoys a soil containing plenty of leaf mould or peat, but above all must be given some of the sharp sand or grit of its native haunts. As the bulbs quickly reproduce themselves both from offsets and self-sown seed, a light mulch during mid-winter will help the bulbs to retain vigour and depth of colour and will provide them with a protective covering which will encourage them to come into bloom when so much appreciated, early in March. A mixture of well-rotted manure and peat or leaf mould would be ideal.

But perhaps the best way with the Chionodoxas indoors is to plant half a dozen bulbs of many species and varieties and colours together in a large seed pan. When taken indoors in the early New Year they will come into bloom late in January. Starting with *C. sardensis*, the various species come into bloom, in turn, right through the later winter and early spring months. Try covering the outside of the pan with a piece of old 'black-out' material, and the effect will astonish you. Or, of course, the same bulbs may be planted in a large but shallow glass or painted pottery bowl. Remember to place some broken crocks along the bottom before filling with compost, to help with drainage; and a good idea is to mix into the compost a small handful of crushed charcoal which will keep the soil sweet over a long period.

Of such distinctive colouring are the Chionodoxa species that I prefer to plant them in drifts, keeping them entirely to themselves. They are rarely troubled by either mice or birds; neither will spring winds harm them. They have, in fact, no drawbacks.

Species

C. gigantea (grandiflora). This species bears large flowers of the

134

clearest sky-blue and is at its best throughout April. The colour is accentuated when planted with *C. gigantea alba*. 5–6 inches.

C. luciliae. This species bears vivid blue flowers with an attractive white eye. The flowers are carried on dainty sprays and are freely producted. This is an excellent species for the alpine garden. There is also a white form, *alba*; *rosea* bears a bloom of deep pink which is even more effective when planted near the others. A new variety of great charm is 'Pink Giant', with spikes of rich shell-pink flowers on nine-inch stems. It is excellent for cutting. As yet the bulbs are expensive at 10*s*. a dozen, but it is a beauty. The *C. luciliae* group bloom during March and April on four-inch stems.

C. sardensis. From Sardinia, and of most striking colour, being similar to the blue of *Gentian sino-ornata*. The flowers are carried in loose sprays and are very freely produced; it comes into bloom early in March and is good for cold frame culture. 4 inches.

C. tmoli. From the Levant, and produces a larger and rather more striking flower than *C. gigantea*, though is not quite so prolific. Blooms early in April. 4 inches.

COLCHICUM

Generally referred to as 'Autumn Crocus', to which they are not even botanically related, though they may resemble the autumn-flowering Crocuses. They are also confused with the Saffron Crocus, *Crocus sativus*, for they are often called the 'Meadow Saffron'. They do, however, bloom from early September and right through October, most of the species being at their best before the true Saffron crocus, *C. sativus*, comes into bloom. Perhaps it is their rather rank foliage borne during spring and early summer that has always told against these plants, for at this time of the year they look most untidy, whereas the true autumn-flowering Crocus is blessed with the dainty grass-like foliage of the spring-flowering species. For this reason they may have suffered through confusion with the Colchicums, when the question of 'autumn crocus' has arisen. Even so the Colchicums, or 'Naked Ladies' as they are called by countrymen, are delightful plants and they should be planted in the shrubbery; in the dell garden; on a grassy bank; or by a stream; and they should be planted in quantity. There they will produce their attractive long cup-shaped flowers when the days are rapidly shortening and will be a delight throughout autumn. I once planted several species along a low wall

135

with several Mossy saxifrages for a soil covering and the effect was delightful. Or try planting the rare yellow *Colchicum luteum* from Kashmir among some plants of the *Juliae* primrose 'Romeo'. This is the only early spring-flowering Colchicum I know, and the only yellow variety. But Mossy saxifrages will be of the greatest value not only as a background to accentuate the colour of the flowers, but also to act in saving the flowers from being splashed by heavy rain.

The leaves will begin to fade with the first warm days of June, and turn an unsightly yellow colour. As with all bulbs, however, they should not be removed until they have completely died back. The bulbs are poisonous, and from them the drug Colchichine is extracted. It is a native plant, though rare, and William Cobbett in his *Rural Rides* has told that he saw it growing in an orchard. The Elizabethans first appreciated it as a garden plant and by Parkinson's time (1629), seventeen forms were known. The bulbs should not be planted where animals may get at them.

Planting

Although the Colchicums seem to do well in almost any well-drained soil, even of poor quality, for they will flourish in a shrubbery of a town garden, they thrive best in one containing plentiful supplies of leaf mould. Being of the same family as the Lilies, they require similar culture. Where leaf mould is not present, fork into the soil a quantity of peat, spent hops or any available humus and do not forget to add some brick rubble. Coarse sand should be liberally sprinkled round the bulbs as they are set just below soil level. July seems to be the best time for planting, for the foliage will by then have died down. The bulbs will then be completely fortified, ready for lifting and replanting. If left undisturbed too long, they will begin to throw up their flower buds which may easily be damaged during replanting. In any case, they should be well established in their new quarters by the time they produce their first flowers towards the end of August. It is interesting to observe that the blooms will remain fresh for several days without having access to moisture. After flowering, the bulb shrinks and a new one forms at its side. The Colchicum is readily distinguished from the Crocus in that it has six stamens whereas the crocus has only three.

Species

   C. agrippinum. This is a very beautiful form, several of the rosy-purple flowers, chequered like those of the Snake'-shead fritillary, arising from each bulb at a height of four inches. To Parkinson it was *C. neapolitanum fritillaricum*—the Chequered Saffron of Naples. It is also known as *C. tessalatum* and *C. Parkinsonii*, and blooms during September and October. It reproduces itself with great vigour and will establish itself almost anywhere.

C. alpinum. It is even more dainty than *C. autumnale*, much resembling a Crocus. It is to be found in the Alps, from whence came those corms growing in my garden. It is the first to bloom, at the beginning of August; its flowers are rosy-lilac throughout, and no more than an inch long.

C. autumnale. This is possibly the only Colchicum to plant in the alpine garden, for its habit is so neat that its foliage should not prove unsightly. The small lavender blooms appear throughout October and November. The white form (*album*) is also most attractive, and there is also a double form, *plenum.* 6 inches.

C. Bornmuelleri magnificum. It was raised by Van Tubergen at Haarlem and is one of the first to bloom. Its very large flowers appear towards the end of August and are of rosy-mauve with a large white centre or base accentuated by the pale green tube. A half-dozen bulbs planted twelve inches apart will produce a most striking display. 8 inches.

C. byzantinum. Named by Clusius in 1601, for it was from Constantinople that he received the corms in 1588; it is the most free-flowering species. It forms its large crimped leaves in spring and bears dainty star-shaped blooms of rose-mauve during August, September and October, as many as twenty flowers appearing in succession and after the foliage has died back. It grows 6 inches high. The late Mr. E. A. Bowles in his *Handbook of Crocus and Colchicum* has told of seeing several bulbs of this plant in the window of a Cornish cottage, flowering entirely without roots. This it will do, if the bulbs are lifted early in August, after the foliage has been removed.

C. callicymbium. This is a quite rare and distinct species to be found in the Botanic Gardens at Cambridge. It is readily distinguished from other Colchicums in that the blooms have a deep violet throat and black anthers, while the leaves appear at the same time as the flowers. 6 inches.

C. luteum. This is the striking yellow 'Crocus' of Turkestan and Afghanistan, the only Colchicum of this colour. Of extremely neat habit, it forms but a few narrow leaves and bears its small golden

137

flowers during February and March. 3 inches. The young flowers will be eaten by slugs if not protected.

C. speciosum. From Persia, and as Farrer in *The English Rock Garden* says: 'One of the most beautiful plants in the world.' *The Century Book of Gardening* reinforces this by describing it as 'a noble flower'. Flowering in late August and into November, it produces its brilliant carmine-purple tulip-like flowers in great profusion. The flowers first appear above the ground as cream coloured, slightly flushed with lilac but soon deepen in colour. It should be planted lavishly in every shrubbery and border. And plant with it the expensive but pure white form, *album*, for a really arresting display; also the striking *atro-rubens*, its light crimson petals having ruby tips.

Of the white form, E. A. Bowles wrote, 'It is one of the most beautiful of all hardy bulbous plants, the snow-white goblets, equal to that of a tulip, standing on soft emerald-green tubes.' He relates that when first introduced it changed hands at 5 guineas a corm, but at Earlham Hall, Norwich, it did so well that 'six roots increased to over five hundred in ten years'. The bulbs of this species are large, at least 4 inches in length and 2 inches in diameter, the flower bud being formed in a groove at the base.

Hybrids

A race of Colchicum hybrids of compact habit and bearing large, refined blooms early in August and over a long period must surely bring a greater popularity to this plant. Outstanding is 'Autumn Queen', with bright rose-coloured flowers with a white base and similar to *C. Bornmuelleri* from which the hybrids were raised by crossing with *C. giganteum*. 'Lilac Wonder' bears a huge bloom of bright carmine-pink, while 'Glory of Heemstede' bears a tasselled, or funnel-shaped, flower. Later to bloom is 'The Giant', with a large flower of lilac pink, with a creamy-white base, on a six-inch stem; and 'Conquest', which has a deep violet flower. Several planted together make an arresting display.

CORYDALIS

For a cold, sunless corner of the garden or rockery there are no more valuable plants. They are worthy of growing if only for their beautiful foliage which is reminiscent of the foliage of the Maidenhair Fern and is of an attractive blue-grey colour. The plants are extremely hardy and will grow well in a damp soil provided it is reasonably well drained in winter. Nor does the soil need to be more fertile than that usually to be found in the average town garden, all of which makes the Corydalis a more than useful plant.

Plant them to the front of the shrubbery or beneath trees, as an edging to a shaded border or in any sunless corner facing north, where the delicacy of their foliage and their long flowering will be greatly appreciated. The plant takes its name from the Greek 'harydalis', a crested lark, which indicates the unusual shape of the flowers. The plants are to be found growing all across Europe and Asia, and bloom from mid-March until June.

The Corydalis is commonly known as 'Fumitory' and while a number of species are propagated by division and from seed, several are best planted in the form of bulbs.

Species

C. angustifolia. From the Caucasus, it must have a shady place and a light soil to produce its pale lavender sprays to advantage. Flowering to a height of about eight inches, it blooms from mid-March until May.

C. bulbosa. Of extremely compact habit, it may be used on the rockery or to edge a small path. It forms masses of grey-green 'fern' above which it bears its rosy-purple flowers during spring. It grows four inches tall and is also known as *C. solida* or 'Bulbous Fumitory'.

C. cava. So named because of its curious hollow bulb from which arise, during April and May, grey fern-like foliage and neat sprays of lilac flowers. There is also a white-flowered form. 8 inches.

C. decipiens. It will grow well in an acid, almost inert soil, forming tufts of attractive grey foliage and magenta-coloured flowers during early summer. 9 inches.

C. densiflora. From Greece and of dwarf habit, covering itself with a mass of rosy-pink flowers in early spring. 6 inches.

C. Wilsonii. Requiring more sunshine than the others, it should be given winter protection in an exposed garden. The bright yellow flowers, delicately marked with green, are of more prostrate form. The foliage is grey-green which accentuates the gold of the bloom, which is at its best during April and May. 8 inches.

CROCUS

It is one of the oldest flowers known to man and was mentioned by Greek writers at least three hundred years before Christ. It was possibly from Greece that the first species reached Britain, this being the autumn-flowering *Crocus sativus*, a plant which grew in abundance along the north coast of Africa and throughout the Middle East, and which has been used in commerce since mediaeval times. Hakluyt, in his *English Voiages*, published in 1581, mentions that the Saffron crocus grew wild in parts of Herefordshire, 'where the best of all England is', and he is not far wrong. During the reign of Edward VI the plant was introduced to that part of Essex now named Saffron Walden, by Sir Thomas Smith, Secretary of State to Edward VI, and a native of the village. His object was to initiate a new industry for his villagers. *Crocus sativus* is a rich purple flower, and saffron is made from the dried stigmas of the bloom. It may still be purchased, four hundred years after its introduction into Essex, the little bulbs (really corms) costing no more than 20s. per hundred.

The Elizabethan writer, Gerard, has referred to the introduction into England of the now so popular yellow spring-flowering Crocus. He calls it 'that pleasant plant sent unto me from Rabinus of Paris'; and says, 'It hath flowers of a most perfect shining yellow colour like a hot glowing coal of fire'.

Later, Parkinson, in his famous *Paradisus* described thirty different varieties, but by 1870 George Maw included sixty species in his publication devoted entirely to the Crocus. Of these a large number may be obtained today. Even towards the end of the reign of Elizabeth I there were a number of varieties known to most gardeners. Shakespeare in *The Tempest*, Act IV, Scene 1, writes:

> *Hail, many-coloured messenger, that ne'er*
> *Dost disobey the wife of Jupiter:*
> *Who with thy saffron wings upon my flowers*
> *Diffusest honey-drops, refreshing showers . . .*

In the reign of the second Elizabeth it is sad to think that so few gardeners grow the lovely autumn-flowering species which will provide brilliancy of colour in the garden from early August until the later-flowering varieties link up with the first of the spring-flowering ones, so providing a continuation of colour from August until the following May.

Soil and situation

The Crocus is a plant which flourishes in both town and country garden. It will grow to perfection in a window-box or around the sides of tubs or boxes holding a specimen plant at the entrance to house or flat. As an edging to a patch or border, or planted in drifts under trees, Crocuses will provide a blaze of colour, but they are also of great value for planting in a tiny garden or courtyard between crazy-paving stones, or on the rockery where their daintiness will be in keeping with their environment; and after flowering, their grass-like leaves will die away almost unnoticed.

In almost any type of soil will they flourish, though they do appreciate one containing a proportion of horticultural peat or leaf mould. The writers of the sixteenth century said that the crocus enjoyed 'some manure': but rather than rank farmyard manure I think that this should be taken to mean humus in general. I have found that hops augmented by a small quantity of old mushroom-bed manure is ideal for Crocus corms, and I use this mixture mixed with a little soil when growing them: in the garden, in pots or bowls, and for a window-box. One thing the Crocus will not tolerate, and that is a stagnant situation; good drainage is essential, and this may be obtained in soils of doubtful nature by incorporating a quantity of coarse sand together with the humus-forming materials. Peat is a most valuable alternative to those materials already mentioned. In particular will the Crocus flourish on a sunny bank from which surplus moisture may readily drain away.

Planting

When planting in grass, in orchard or lawn, a small amount of humus should be placed in the cavity formed when the turf has been removed. This should be done by making a firm cut with a spade on three sides. The turf should then be lifted and rolled over the side which has not been cut, exactly like a box lid on hinges. A turf of a depth of 4 inches should be removed, a size which may easily be gauged with a little practice. Into the cavity should be placed a little humus material and some coarse sand, and into this the corms should be pressed, flat side downwards. Six corms of the 7 cm. size should be placed under each turf, which should be replaced into its original position and made quite firm by treading. The whole operation takes but a few minutes, and a large area may be planted up in an hour or so.

Where the Crocus is planted in a rockery or along the edging of a path, or between crazy paving, it should be planted three inches deep by means of a trowel. Plant in clusters of self colours or species to obtain the best effect, spacing the corms the same distance apart as they are deep in the ground.

The spring-flowering species should be planted in October; those that bloom in autumn and winter are planted in May or June. By giving care to one's choice of species, it will be possible to enjoy colour almost the whole year round, setting out the corms in short grass beneath trees, in the shrubbery or about the rockery, and the corms may also be planted in troughs and window boxes; and, of course, in pots and bowls for the alpine house and house itself. Crocuses grow three to four inches high, the flowers having a long perianth tube instead of a stalk (stem).

If the Crocus has a drawback, it is that in some years of prolonged bad weather the winter- and early spring-flowering species may be cut down by cold winds; so plant in a sunny nook. Also, they may receive too much attention from birds, which find a sweetened moisture at the base of the flowers. The autumn-flowering varieties which are in bloom at a season of plenty rarely suffer in this way, and of the spring species I have found that it is almost entirely the yellow varieties that are liable to attack. If you have them growing in large numbers, 'Glitterbangs', patented by the Chase Protected Cultivation Limited, prove most valuable, and they may later be used for protecting strawberries, and, even later, autumn-sown seeds in the open. But for those with only small groups, the old method of placing black thread (rather than cotton) around the plants when in bud will prove effective. Do not wait until the flowers are fully showing colour before protecting, for the whole display may be destroyed in a few hours, and there is nothing more disappointing.

Mice, too, may prove troublesome to newly planted crocus corms, especially where a hard winter is being experienced and there is precious little food about. A non-poisonous preparation of a proprietary brand placed about the ground where the corms have been planted will keep this pest under control. The Crocus-lover who has room in the garden to plant in large numbers will find that a cat is quite the best deterrent to both mice and birds and a brilliant display can be expected with certainty where a cat is keeping watch.

MINIATURE BULBS: ALPHABETICAL LIST

Species and Varieties

C. asturicus. From the Pyrenees, it produces its lilac blooms, striped dark blue at the base, during October and November. As with *C. nudiflorus*, the leaves appear after the flowers.

C. cancellatus. The white form *albus* is one of the most beautiful of the autumn-flowering Crocuses, the large silvery-white blooms being enhanced by the vivid orange anthers. The corms are sold as food in the markets of Damascus.

C. Karduchorum. One of the finest of all the Crocus species, and though discovered in 1859 is only now to be obtained commercially. It bears large flowers with broad petals, pointed at the tips, and which are of an exquisite shade of lavender-pink enhanced by the white throat. It blooms during October and has small, narrow leaves.

C. Kashmiriana. A rare variety which may be found at high altitudes in Kashmir. It produces its rich pale blue flowers in October and makes an arresting display.

C. medius. May be seen at its best along the Southern coast of France, but it grows equally well in the cooler climate of Britain. Its rich, deep violet blooms are marked at the throat with deep purple rays, and its orange-red stigmas makes it a most striking species. The leaves, too, are striking, having a wide central white line. It blooms during October.

C. nudiflorus. Much like *C. zonatus*, its lilac-mauve flowers appear before the leaves, in early October. It is a free and continuous-flowering plant, native of the Pyrenees, and is Parkinson's *Crocus perenaeus purpureus*. The plant increases by means of stolons which take about three years to grow into a flowering-size corm. The Yorkshire naturalist, William Crump, has described how the plant has become naturalised on the grassy hillsides around Halifax; and it was his opinion that at one time many of the hillside farms were the property of the Knights of St. John, who brought the corms back with them from the Mediterranean.

C. pulchellus. It blooms during October, its lavender-blue flowers having white anthers and an orange throat. The new variety, 'Zephyr', is outstandingly lovely, with large white blooms shaded on the inside with grey.

C. Salzmannii. Though its natural habitat is Southern Spain and Tangier, it is a vigorous, hardy Crocus forming the largest corm of all the species, and bearing its silvery-lilac flowers, after its leaves, early in November.

C. sativus. The true Saffron Crocus, in bloom during October and noted for the dense yellow deposit on the stigmas, of which the Elizabethan writer Gerard said: 'Moderate use of it is good for the head . . . it shaketh off drowsie sleep and maketh men merrie'. It would also be grown entirely for its lovely purple-pink flower, which is streaked a deeper purple and which remains in bloom for a long period.

C. speciosus. This is a magnificent late-September-flowering Crocus remaining long in bloom and being happy in all soils and in any position in the garden. The large, almost globular, violet-blue flowers, are feathered with crimson and made brighter by their orange-red stigma. The form '*Aitchisonii*' is especially fine, the long tapering blooms, which appear in October, being of a lovely shade of China blue; while *albus* has pure white blooms with the same bright orange stigma. The new 'Oxonian' has a large globular bloom of dark blue, the interior of pale blue.

C. zonatus. It blooms in September, with the mushrooms, the thin tubular lilac pink blooms zoned with orange spots at the throat, and with their white stigmas, appearing before the leaves. It is also known as *C. Kotschyanus* and is native to the Lebanon and Syria. It forms a large flat corm and needs a well-drained position.

WINTER-FLOWERING

C. Boryi. Flowering in November and December and producing dainty blooms of creamy-white, with white anthers, this species is seen at its best when planted with *C. asturicus.* It is more tender than most species and should be grown in the South or preferably in the alpine house.

C. imperati. One of the most handsome and valuable of all the Crocus species, it comes into bloom at the year's end and continues through the bleakest days until March. The outer petals are fawn or biscuit coloured, feathered with violet. There is also a pure white form, *montanus*, found near Naples.

C. Korolkowi. It comes into bloom early in January and continues until March, the flowers being star-shaped, while the brilliant yellow colour of the dainty blooms is much appreciated at this time. The exterior of the bloom is beautifully stippled with bronze and the inner surface has a varnished appearance.

39. Miniature bulbs set out beneath a sunny wall

40. *Crocus speciosus* (Autumn flowering). The blooms open in the warmth of the sun showing the beautiful purple veining of the lilac petals

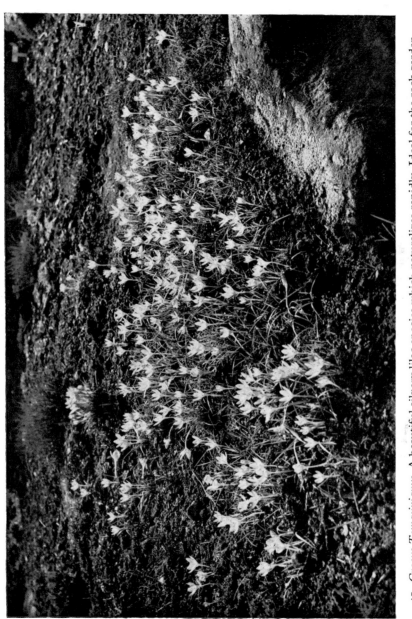

41. *Crocus Tomasinianus.* A beautiful silvery lilac species which naturalizes rapidly. Ideal for the rock garden

42. *Crocus dalmaticus.* Silvery lavender-blue flowers with bright orange stamens. A fine species for pots or outdoors. Flowers February–March

43. *Crocus dalmaticus*

C. laevigatus. A most valuable species from the Caspian Sea area, producing star-like flowers or rich violet during the bleakest days of December and January. It has a potent scent.

C. longiflorus. Though native to Sicily and Malta, it blooms during November when damp foggy weather frequently covers the land, and when colour in the garden is most appreciate. The long lavender tubes with their scarlet stigmas have a rich perfume.

C. niveus. A most outstanding variety, first recognized as a distinct species by the late E. A. Bowles in 1900. The flowers are large and globular, the pure white segments having a vivid orange throat. The vividness is accentuated by the scarlet stigmas. It is a hardy Crocus, coming into bloom as the snow melts, towards the year's end, and continuing until March.

C. ochroleucus. A native of Galilee, this is a most outstanding November- and December-flowering crocus, the dainty creamy-white blooms with their white stigmas providing a pleasing foil for the purple- and blue-flowered species, especially *C. laevigatus* and *C. longiflorus*, in bloom at the same time.

C. Tournefortii. A rare Crocus, it bears a large bloom of a unique shade of warm rosy-lilac with a rich orange throat, and is at its loveliest during the dark November days. It is found only in the Greek Archipelago and should be given a sheltered place facing south. Where happy, it will increase rapidly.

SPRING-FLOWERING

C. ancyrensis. The tiny bloom looks so delicate as it opens to the early February sunshine but these Crocuses have a remarkable ability for standing up to severe weather. They should, however, be given some protection from the wind and are best planted in nooks about a rockery; on a grassy bank facing the sun; or as an edging to a path, where the blooms of deepest golden-orange will be produced in great profusion.

C. Balansae. First discovered near Smyrna, it blooms during March and is one of the smallest and most fairylike of all Crocuses. The best form is 'Zwanenburg Variety', its marigold-orange blooms suffused with mahogany on the outside, and stippled with bronze.

C. biflorus. From Greece, with attractive silvery white flowers, striped with blue. Very free-flowering, ideal under trees, and at its best in March. There are several forms of this species in which

C. biflorus 'Weldeni', a pale grey, and *pusillus*, white with an orange throat, from Yugoslavia, are outstanding and equally free flowering.

C. candidus. It blooms during April and comes from the Levant. The form *mountainii* is interesting. It bears freely, small globular flowers of richest orange. Seedlings raised by Van Tubergen had a yellow ground and were styled *sub-flavus*.

C. chrysanthus. This is the large 'Golden Flowered Crocus' from Greece and Asia Minor and is one of the finest of all, coming into bloom towards the end of February and continuing until April. As to colour, it is the most variable species of all, an outstanding variety being 'E. A. Bowles', named by Van Tubergen, its raiser, after our greatest authority on the Crocus. It has a large bloom of buttercup yellow, tinted with grey at the base. Plant with it the new 'Blue Pearl', its soft pearly-blue flowers having an attractive yellow centre. Equally desirable is the free-flowering 'Cream Beauty', its globular flowers of a satisfying shade of soft creamy-yellow. And do not forget the magnificent 'Peace', its huge snow-white blooms veined with slate blue on the outside. The late E. A. Bowles himself named many lovely hybirds of his own raising after birds.

C. corsicus. This is quite a rare species but is most free-flowering and extremely handsome with its cream-coloured flowers feathered on the outside with mauve. It blooms during March.

C. dalmaticus. Lilac, yellow throat, flower tube about two inches long. Flowers February to March.

C. Fleischeri. This species should be planted on a grassy bank where the vivid red anthers may be seen through the almost transparent white star-shaped petals. Or plant it for contrast about clusters of *Juliae* primrose 'Wanda' or 'Marie Crousse', along the edge of a path or border. It is in flower from February until April.

C. minimus. This is one of the smallest species; the flowers are lavender, shaded buff on the outside, and only one-and-a-half inches high. It is a charming little plant, but shy and thus costly.

C. olivieri. Found on the Island of Chios in the Aegean, it is the latest of all the Crocuses to bloom, being at its best during April and well into May. With *C. minimus* it is the smallest. For all that, its brilliant orange flowers are most striking beneath young trees, especially those of the *Cupressus* group.

C. Sieberi. Similar to *Fleischeri* but at its best throughout February. Its rich lavender-blue blooms of delicate golden throat make this a delightful Crocus for the cold greenhouse when grown in pans, or for the window box. The new variety 'Violet Queen' has globular flowers of deep violet-blue.

C. susianus. The striking 'Cloth of Gold' crocus which reached this country from the shores of the Black Sea in 1587. It comes into bloom at the end of March, the glossy golden blooms being striped with brown on the exterior, while the narrow segments taper to a point. It is also known as *C. angustifolius.*

C. Tomasinianus. A native of Bulgaria, it is in bloom during February and March. It was named after the botanist Muzio de Tomasini, of Trieste, and is one of the best of all. The long thin tubes are of a brilliant shade of sapphire blue, and the new variety 'Taplow Ruby' has large flowers of deepest ruby-red. It increases rapidly both from its cormlets and from seed and is most valuable planted about a shrubbery, or as an edging to a path where it need not be disturbed.

C. vernus albus. The 'Snow Crocus' of the Alps which replaces the snow with carpets of creamy-white trumpets. Plant with it the new 'Haarlem Gem' which also blooms in March and bears lilac-blue flowers of great substance.

C. versicolor. It is to be found in numerous forms along the Riviera, the most outstanding being that known as the 'Cloth of Silver' Crocus, its silvery-white blooms feathered by purple-crimson.

The Dutch hybrids

Here is a selection of the best modern hybrids, descendants of *C. vernus,* that are an essential element of the Crocus garden. Most of them produce larger blooms than the other species, so they are at their best during March and early April when massed under orchard or parkland trees or in the short grass of lawn or bank. They are excellent, too, for pot culture in cold greenhouse or home, flowering when most of the spring-flowering species are over.

'Early Perfection.' Almost a pure navy blue and with a very large bloom. At its best early in March.

'Enchantress.' Bears a huge bloom of real Wedgwood blue.

'Jeanne D'Arc.' Produces a huge bloom of purest white.

'Kathleen Parlow.' A magnificent white with a striking pale yellow throat.

'Little Dorrit.' The dainty globular blooms are of a charming shade of silvery-blue.

'Mammoth.' Recognized as the finest of the yellow varieties, producing a huge cup-shaped bloom, and in flower over a long period.

'Nigger Boy.' The deepest purple, to follow 'The Sultan.'

'Pallas.' An old variety introduced in 1914, producing white flowers heavily striped pale blue.

'Paulus Potter.' A striking variety, the huge blooms being of rich, glossy ruby-red.

'Queen of the Blues.' Produces a large refined bloom of soft sky blue.

'Remembrance.' The colour of the old-fashioned lilac, and remains in bloom for a long period.

'Striped Beauty.' A popular novelty, grey-white, striped with porcelain blue.

'The Sultan.' Very deep purple of perfect shape.

'Vanguard.' It is the first of the Dutch hybrids to bloom, the colour being pale lavender, flushed with grey on the exterior.

'White Lady.' Possibly the largest white, and grows well anywhere.

CYCLAMEN

They are happiest in shade and though the corms enjoy a leafy soil, they grow best where the soil has a high lime content. Where lime is not present naturally then a liberal dressing of lime rubble (mortar) should be given at planting time. This will also encourage adequate drainage without which the corms will decay during the dormant winter period. Where the soil is none too friable, incorporate plenty of peat or leaf mould and a small quantity of either sand or grit.

A permanent position should be chosen for the planting of the corms, preferably beneath mature trees, in those pockets often formed by the exposed roots and where the plants, when in bloom, will receive protection from cold winds. Here, too, neither grass nor weeds will be troublesome and the plants will reveal their full beauty. The corms will quickly increase in size, while self-sown seedlings will augment the display; so do not plant too closely together.

Several corms of each species should be planted separately around each tree, eighteen inches apart and only just covered with compost. The corms should be pressed into the soil which has previously been made firm by treading, and over the corms a little prepared compost should be scattered. As it becomes established, the corm will tend to push itself out of the soil and thus it is important to provide it with a dressing each year, composed of soil, leaf mould and lime rubble.

The most suitable month for planting the corms is July, the exceptions being *C. europeum* and *C. graecum*, which will be in full bloom at this time. *C. europaeum* also differs from the other species in that it enjoys deep planting, up to six inches deep where the soil is light and friable. Always remember to plant the rounded or smooth side downwards, and keep the corms moist until they have become established. A number of the species may not bloom the first year, but they will make up for this by the mottled beauty of their foliage. The blooms, which hover like butterflies and remain fresh for several weeks, will be enhanced if ivy is allowed to trail about the plants.

Growing from seed

Where self-sown seedlings are not readily obtainable, seedlings may be raised by artificial means. One authority on alpine plants has suggested sowing hardy Cyclamen seed on a layer of limestone chippings, and I have found this to be an excellent method. Boxes or seed pans may be used, pans being more suitable, for the seedlings are better if allowed to remain in the pans for a full twelve months, where they will grow on slowly all the time. My method is to mix together a compost of equal parts of peat and rotted turf loam, then over this I place in the pans a layer of limestone chippings which have been pulverized but not too finely. Directly on to the chippings the seed is sown, thus right from the beginning the plant is provided with its lime requirements.

As with most alpine plants, the seed should be as fresh as possible when sown, and as most species flower between September and April, early summer is generally taken to be the most suitable time. The seed should germinate readily if the pans are covered with a sheet of glass and allowed to stand in a cold frame or greenhouse, shielded from the summer sunshine. Careful watering is necessary and, especially throughout the following winter where the plants will remain in their seed pans in a cold frame, partial protection from severe frosts by a covering of sacks or straw. The following spring should see the plants set out into individual pots of the 2½-inch size and still in a cold frame they will be grown on for another twelve months. They will then have formed a small corm which will be ready for planting out during the early summer. This may take another twelve months to become thoroughly established before flowering, after which, in a soil they like, they will produce more and more bloom each season.

For pot culture

The greenhouse Cyclamen is not the only one which will bloom indoors, for many of the dainty hardy species are equally obliging; and where a heated greenhouse is not available, they will prove most valuable for display throughout the entire winter period. What they must be given is a compost containing not only lime rubble but also a large quantity of peat or leaf mould. In fact the compost should be made up of 2 parts peat (or leaf mould), 1 part loam, 1 part lime rubble. This should be thoroughly mixed and well moistened, and for the hardy Cyclamen an earthenware seed pan is far the best container. Six corms of different species, or whichever selection is required, should be pressed into the compost, which has been made very firm, yet is still springy when the corms are pressed in, the top of the corms being level with the top of the compost. Planting should be done in early October and the pans may be stood in a cold shaded frame or placed directly into a cold greenhouse. They will require only very occasional waterings, otherwise the crowns will tend to rot should the weather be dull and misty. Depending upon the species, they will come into bloom at Christmas and extend their flowering season right through the winter and spring. A single corm set in a 2½-inch pot will also provide a charming addition to the dressing-table, for they will grow well in a window, or they may be taken indoors from a frame or greenhouse as soon as the first buds are seen.

Plants may also be lifted with care from the rockery or from around the roots of trees at the appropriate time, a mature corm being large enough to fill a 60-size pot. In a cool room it will produce its dainty blooms over a period of several weeks.

Species

WINTER-FLOWERING

C. alpinum. I have never been able to obtain this lovely species for my garden but have frequently admired it in a friend's collection, where it is always in bloom on Christmas Day, its pure white flowers attractively blotched with purple. 3 inches.

C. Atkinsii. It resembles *C. coum* not only in form but also in its flowering period. In a sheltered position it will come into bloom before Christmas and remain colourful until the end of March. The leaves are mottled and the blooms are larger than those of *C. coum* and of a paler shade of magenta. 4 inches.

C. coum. Discovered on the Island of Cos, Asia Minor, it forms a corm which is flatter than that of most other species. It comes into bloom at the turn of the year and continues until Easter; the pretty short-petalled flowers are of bright magenta-red and held above shining bottle-green leaves. There is also a white form, *album*, blotched with maroon, and a deep pink form, *roseum*. 3 inches.

SPRING-FLOWERING

C. libanoticum. From Syria, and an exquisite plant, having grey-green leaves which appear in autumn and bearing masses of violet-pink flowers during March and early April. The blooms are deliciously fragrant. The corms are expensive and are difficult to establish, being less hardy than the other species. 6 inches.

C. repandum. Like *C. coum*, its corm is quite flat, while its leaves are broad and ivy-shaped and beautifully marbled with silver. It is the most inexpensive species and possibly the most attractive, for its vivid crimson blooms are held above the foliage on six-inch stems. It blooms with great freedom during April and May. Also wrongly known as *C. vernum*. 6 inches.

SUMMER-FLOWERING

C. europeum. From the lower shopes of the Alps comes this charming plant which enjoys deep planting and produces, before its handsome silver-marbled foliage, its sweetly scented flowers, rosy-red on four-inch stems. Happiest in partial shade it blooms from July to October, an established corm often producing more than a hundred flowers. Plant it in March near *C. coum* and there will be an almost continuous display of bloom from the New Year through spring and summer until *C. neapolitanum* takes over in early autumn to continue the show until almost the year's end. The plant retains its foliage for most of the year. 4 inches.

C. graecum. It is most valuable in that it bridges the gap between *C. europaeum* and the true autumn-flowering species. From the end of July until almost the end of September it bears its pretty pink flowers above large heart-shaped leaves. 4 inches.

AUTUMN-FLOWERING

C. africanum. It also has large heart-shaped leaves, zoned with silver, and bears its blush-pink flowers splashed with purple from early September until early November. The leaves are attractively waved at the edges, and the flower petals are long and twisted. Natives of North Africa, the corms are less hardy than others and should be given a protective mulch after flowering. 4 inches.

C. cilicium. It bears a large medium-green leaf which has a large heart-shaped zone of silver, and pretty pink flowers with attractively twisted petals throughout autumn. It is one of the most free-flowering and graceful of all the hardy Cyclamen and is ideal for the rockery or for planting in a trough garden. 3 inches.

C. neapolitanum. Where it is happy, the corms will increase in size for fifty or more years until they have become as large as a saucer. The plants require almost no moisture so long as they are growing in shade. As the tuber increases in size, so does it produce more bloom, several tubers planted closely together providing a rich display throughout autumn. The tubers will greatly appreciate a yearly mulch. The long ivy-shaped leaves are heavily marbled with white and, as they appear from late in autumn until early summer, provide a pleasing ground cover for Chionodoxas and Snowdrops. The blooms, which vary in colour from pale to deep pink, appear in September before the leaves. There is also a beautiful white form, *album.* 4 inches.

ERANTHIS

With its golden cups of the utmost brilliance nestling in a frill of bright green, the Winter Aconite is a most colourful plant; and besides its earliness its claim to distinction must lie in its ability to thrive in almost any soil and in damp, shady places. In the town shrubbery, in soil polluted by fumes and soot deposits, how well the *Eranthis* flourishes! Even a fall of snow seems to have no effect on their hardiness for as soon as a thaw sets in and the snow departs, there the vivid yellow and green flowers are ready to greet the sedate rays of the winter sun. Nor do they mind a heavy, damp soil. This does not mean they will flourish in a water-logged soil, but a soil with a high clay content, which has been brought into as favourable a condition as possible by the incorporation of some peat and sand, gravel or grit, will grow the Winter Aconite to perfection. And many a dull corner, too, may be illumined by the golden glow of this flower. Holding their blooms full face to the sky, even a very few will give an attractive display, but where possible, plant freely, in the cracks of crazy paving, along the edges of a window box, in a trough or tub, down the side of a path, under trees and shrubs and in the lawn or in any grass which is kept short; and here they look delightful mingling with *Galanthus Elwesii*, which blooms during January and February.

The Winter Aconite is also a charming plant for naturalising in the woodland garden and planting about a lawn or orchard where the grass is kept short. Flowering so early, its foliage will have died away before the lawn is cut late in spring.

Planting

The small bulbs should be planted as near to September 1st as possible. They bloom very early, so should be given ample time to form a strong root system. The depth to plant should be about two inches, but as with all small bulbs, it is better to err on the side of shallow planting. If the soil is unduly heavy, sprinkle under and over the bulbs, before replacing the soil or turf, a handful of a mixture of peat and coarse sand.

Species and varieties

E. cilicica. This species blooms during February. It bears deep buttercup-yellow flowers set in a ruff of bronze. It multiplies freely and is the best species for massing in grass.

E. 'Guinea Gold'. This is a new hybrid Winter Aconite, the only one which carries a distinct perfume. It bears deep golden flowers and bronze serrated foliage and is at its best early in March. As yet it is expensive.

E. hyemalis. A native of Europe and extremely hardy, blooming in protected places very early in the New Year. The flowers are lemon yellow and the ruff is deep green. The flowers open no more than 2–3 inches above the soil level.

ERYTHRONIUM

This is among the most beautiful of all spring flowers. *Erythronium dens-canis* is known as the Dog's Tooth Violet on account of its long, pearly bulb or tuber which greatly resembles a dog's tooth. The early Roman writers knew it well, for its native country is Italy. The great advantage of this plant is its liking for a cool, shady position. Plant the Aconite in a slightly damp location, the Crocus and Chionodoxa in the sun, the Snowdrop in partial shade; and in a position of almost total shade, sheltered from the prevailing winds but where the sun does not often reach, e.g. a north or east border, a shrubbery or about the roots of trees, plant the Dog's Tooth Violets. They flourish exceedingly if they are given a soil containing a high proportion of peat or leaf mould; in fact, they will be happy only in such a soil.

Not only will the plants flourish in a shrubbery which contains plenty of leaf mould (they are never at their best in the usual town garden with its soil almost entirely devoid of humus), but they make a brilliant display (in my garden) under a row of silver birch trees, planted on a bank which slopes away from the sun, against the trunks of the trees. There against the silver-white bark and in grass which is kept closely cut around the plants, they thrive and bloom to perfection, shielded from the hot summer sun by the foliage of the trees and by the grass which is then allowed to grow.

By a stream or pond, provided the ground is not too moist, the plants will do well. They look particularly attractive planted amongst primulas of the *Juliae* types. With *Primula Juliae* itself, plant *Erythronium dens-canis*, 'Snowflake', which will produce pure white flowers on stems held just above the dwarf-growing Primula. Or reverse the contrast, and plant *E. dens-canis* 'Franz Hals' with Primrose 'Harbinger', an early white, or even with the yellow-flowering woodland Primrose. Or plant with *Viola biflora*, which is very tiny, and comes into bloom about April 1st, with tiny golden blooms, and like the *Erythronium* loving a cool, shady position; but here plant under trees where no grass grows or its charm will be shrouded.

Planting

Care of the bulbs is most important for they will quickly deteriorate if out of the ground too long or exposed to sunshine or wind. If allowed to become too dry they will shrivel, and no amount of careful planting will nurse them back to health. September is the ideal month for lifting, for then the weather is cool and if possible the bulbs should be lifted and planted within a few days while still moist. They will then quickly become established and increase rapidly. Even more than most bulbs they appreciate a regular yearly mulch with peat given during August. To guard against over-dryness during summer the bulbs should be planted three inches deep.

If the soil is not disturbed, the plants will naturally sow their seed and increase rapidly. Or they may be increased by sowing seed in shallow pans or boxes during May in a cold frame which is shaded from strong sunlight. Sow the seed into a compost containing 2 parts peat or leaf mould, 1 part loam, 1 part coarse sand. Merely press the seed into the compost, water thoroughly, and cover with a sheet of glass. The seed should germinate evenly and when large enough to handle the seedlings are transplanted to boxes and allowed to remain there over winter, before being transferred to a shady position the following April. There they will bloom in two years' time when thoroughly established. It is not advisable to lift and divide the clumps other than when they become absolutely overcrowded; and to prevent damage to the bulbs when exposed to the air, any dividing should be done on a calm day.

Species

E. californicum. This is a most striking spring flower. The creamy white, bell-shaped blooms, which are blotched with orange and brown, are carried on twelve-inch stems. The foliage, too, is attractive being deep green mottled with brown. There is a form, *helenae*, which has fragrant petals of white, lined with deep yellow. Both are expensive and should be well cared for at planting time. They flower during March and April.

E. citrinum. Also a connoisseur's plant, and exceedingly lovely, the lemon-coloured flowers being carried on nine-inch stems. They remain in bloom over a long period.

E. dens-canis. Dog's Toothed, it is named from the shape of the bulb. The variety 'Franz Hals' is of a richer red-violet shade. It is carried on six-inch stems also red, and the leaves are mottled. Blooms mid-March to mid-April. There are two other very pleasing varieties, 'Pink Perfection', with flowers of a bright shell pink and 'Snowflake', purest white. Together they make a lovely trio for the shady garden or on a rockery facing away from the south.

E. Hendersonii. Found growing naturally in the Oregon district of the U.S.A., this is a dwarf edition and bears its flowers of a clear lavender in great profusion during April. The flowers are almost identical with those of a Hardy Cyclamen. 4 inches.

E. revolutum. Flowers very early in March as the first of its species; the most expensive, too. The white flowers are unique in that the petals are rolled back, revealing a crimson centre. It increases rapidly. From California, the main breeding-round of the *Erythronium*, it grows to nine inches.

E. tuolumnense. A plant for the connoisseur, producing its rich daffodil-coloured blooms on twelve-inch stems throughout March.

This is a hardy species with shiny unspotted green leaves, and is happiest when planted in short grass under deciduous trees.

FRITILLARIA

There is no more beautiful plant for naturalising than the Snake's Head Fritillary, *F. meleagris*, which will beautify an orchard or coppice with its dancing bells just when the trees are coming into blossom and leaf. With luck, the blooms may be found about the water meadows along the Thames Valley, for the plants appreciate moist conditions and are happy in sunshine or partial shade. In his *Paradisus*, Parkinson describes a dozen species and refers to it as the 'Ginny Hen Flower', 'the variety of colours in the flower agreeing with the feathers of that bird'. Parkinson tells us that the plant was also known as *Narcissus Caparonius*, named after Noel Caperon, an apothecary of Orleans who first discovered it. It was also called 'Lilianarcissus', for it was thought to be a cross between the Lily and Daffodil. At the beginning of the seventeenth century the fritillaries were held in high esteem, 'to be an ornament for the gardens of the curious lovers of these delights'.

Planting

The bulbs should be planted in autumn four inches deep and six inches apart, with a little sand or peat sprinkled over the bulbs to prevent decaying. They should be planted in grass which will not be cut until the foliage has died back in July or August. As pot plants they are quite delightful, and should be grown in the alpine house or in the window of a cool room, for they like plenty of light.

Species and varieties

F. citrina. This species is becoming more and more difficult to obtain. This is tragic for it is one of the most delightful plants of the garden. It blooms throughout May, bearing its pale lemon-yellow bells above attractive grey foliage. The outside of the bloom often takes on bronzy tints. It grows only six inches tall and so is ideal for a rockery and pot culture.

F. meleagris. Producing its dainty drooping bell-shaped blooms on twelve-inch stems during early summer, it is at its best in the orchard and wild garden, planted in groups, the lovely pure white *alba* being

156

enchanting when planted with the deep purple *nigra*. There is also a form, *praecox*, which blooms early in April. Of named varieties, 'Aphrodite' has large pure white flowers, free of any markings; 'Orion' has deep claret-red blooms, finely mottled; 'Artemis' has flowers of an unusual shade of greyish-mauve prettily chequered. All grow to a height of about nine inches.

F. pudica. A delightful little rockery plant with charming little bells of clear golden yellow on four-inch stems through the months spring.

GALANTHUS

Though the Scilly Islander may enjoy his Daffodils when the Scottish and North Country gardens are encased in snow and ice, these more exposed parts have been compensated by nature in that nowhere else does the Snowdrop bloom in such profusion. Of all bulbous plants, the Galanthus most resents any degree of forcing, and in the Peak District of Derbyshire, along the exposed East Coast of Yorkshire, in Northumberland and along the banks of the Clyde and Forth, the Snowdrop may be seen whitening the ground again as soon as the snow has departed.

Surprisingly, the plant is not native to this country, and it was not until the beginning of the seventeenth century that we find any mention of it. In Southern Europe it is known as the 'Milkflower'.

Where planted in the South, the bulbs should be given a northerly aspect and some shade so that the plants may be kept as cool as possible. For this reason, the snowdrop is happiest where growing in grass which protects both bulbs and blooms. Or they may be planted around the base of mature trees, where the bulbs will receive protection from the summer sunshine and the blooms from March winds.

Planting

For massing, a 3-cm. bulb will be large enough to ensure a display of bloom the first year. If obtained smaller, they may not produce a flower until two years after planting. For window boxes and pots indoors always use a 5-cm bulb., though the cost will be almost double. The bulbs should be light in colour and quite firm when received; a soft bulb may be a diseased bulb or one that has not been correctly dried. The time for planting is around September 1st, but not too late in the month, while those that flower before Christmas should be planted during May. All bulbs should be allowed plenty of time to make ample root growth before they come into bloom.

Snowdrops are not fussy as to soil, provided it is well drained and does not contain too much clay. An average loamy soil is ideal, one containing a small amount of leaf mould, and I have found that the bulbs do appreciate a mulch with decayed manure and peat given every other year during June, when the foliage has died down.

Though a bulb of good quality will quickly establish itself, division of the clumps immediately after flowering in April is even more satisfactory. The bulbs will then produce a profusion of flowers in their first winter. If a light mulch is given early in June immediately after the foliage has died down it will help to conserve moisture in the bulb during a hot summer, which is vitally important, for the Snowdrop dislikes both over-dryness and over-wetness. The bulbs may be divided when established and whenever the clumps become over-large; in this way they are easily increased, and they will also increase themselves from self-sown seed.

The Snowdrops may be planted in the shrubbery, as an edging to a path, or under any forest trees, but I think they look their best in short grass, especially in clusters about the lawn or in other grass which is kept short. Flowering and dying down before a lawn is first cut in April, unlike the Daffodil the Snowdrop does not suffer from the removal of its foliage before the sap has run back and fortified the bulb for next season's flowering.

They are ideal subjects for the rockery, also planted with the winter-flowering Crocus in pockets containing peat or leaf mould and a little decayed manure. Wherever possible they should be given whatever protection can be provided to guard against cold prevailing winds which may retard flowering of the mid-winter species. Plant them around the trunks of large trees or behind a hedge or wall or in a part of the garden which may receive some protection from severe winds.

Like all the smaller bulbs, the Snowdrop should not be planted too deeply; three inches is the maximum. A trowel should be used; or, if planting on a lawn, it will be better to use a spade and to roll up a square foot of turf, set about nine to ten bulbs, and firmly replace the turf by treading.

Species and varieties

G. Allenii. A later spring-flowering variety, unique in that its leaves are the largest both in length and width of all the snowdrop species. The blooms are egg-shaped and of pure milk-white. 4 inches.

G. byzantinus. A native of Turkey and apart from its dainty habit it is one of the earliest to bloom, flowering from the end of November until mid-January, when *G. nivalis* succeeds it. Its large white flowers have an interesting green spot on each petal. 4 inches.

G. 'Colesbourne'. Like the tall-growing Arnott's Seedling, this new Snowdrop received an Award of Merit from the Royal Horticultural Society in 1951. Though dwarf in habit and ideal for window boxes, pots and cold house culture, the flowers are of great substance, frilled white and green. 4 inches.

G. Elwesii. One of the later-flowering Snowdrops, at its best early in March, and one of the finest of all varieties. The flowers are carried on long stems and are extremely attractive, with deep green markings on the petal tips and at the base. The foliage is of a delicate grey. 9 inches.

G. imperati. Naturally found in the Naples district of Italy, it produces its long-stemmed flowers at Christmas and is an excellent variety for cloche and pot work. The best form is *Atkinsii*. 6 inches.

G. latifolius. The best variety for a rockery, being very small and producing a thinly-petalled green-tipped flower late in March. 3 inches.

G. nivalis. This is the snowdrop we all know for very early spring-flowering. It does well in pots and under cloches. The form *viridispice* has green-tipped petals; *flore plena* is the double variety, very lovely, but not quite so early. The form 'Straffan Variety' is quite outstanding, the blooms when fully open measuring two inches in diameter. The icy-white blooms are marked with green on the inner petals. The leaves are broad and strap-like, and each bulb will produce two blooms. 5–6 inches.

G. Olgae. From Greece, and particularly useful because it will bloom throughout October. Prefers a dry position and is generally at its best on a rockery. Exquisitely shaped and entirely white flowers. 6 inches.

G. plicatus. From the Crimea region of Russia, and follows *G. nivalis* in flowering-time. It bears huge pure white flowers and grey-green leaves and is most prolific in sowing its own seed. 8 inches.

HAEMANTHUS. See Chapter 11.

HOMERIA. See Chapter 11.

HYACINTH

The true Miniature hyacinths may be likened both to the Scillas and the Muscari and may be said to possess the outstanding qualities of both these plants. Louise Wilder has described these delightful flowers as being 'endowed with a gentle grace', and Reginald Farrer, in *The English Rock Garden*, has said of *H. amethystinus*, 'without rivalry or comparison, it stands supreme amongst the loveliest bulbs we have, and yet is so rarely seen'. Why it is so rarely planted is difficult to imagine, for the bulbs cost only 20*s*. per hundred and may be used for massing beneath trees and in the shrubbery, for planting about an alpine lawn, or along a path. They are also useful for small pots, or in a window box, where their fragrance will be fully appreciated.

The flower spikes are produced during March and April and are packed with tiny globular bells like those of the Grape Hyacinth. They like a position to which the spring sunshine may penetrate and a well-drained, sandy soil. Plant in October, spacing the bulbs three to four inches apart and planting them three inches deep.

Species

H. amethystinus. It has the habit of the squill but is more graceful, the amethyst-blue bells being spaced evenly apart almost for the entire length of stem to give the appearance of a miniature montbretia. Its upright, rush-like foliage also adds to its grace. The flowers are excellent for cutting for small vases. A native of the Pyrenees, it has been grown in Britain for more than two hundred years, and yet remains sadly neglected. William Robinson in his *English Flower Garden* fully agrees with Farrer, and suggests that 'instead of growing a dozen bulbs, it should be grown by the hundred'. 8 inches.

H. azureus. It much more resembles a Grape Hyacinth than does *H. amethystinus*, for the tiny globular flowers of azure blue, and those of its white counterpart, *albus*, cluster together at the end of short stems. It increases rapidly from bulbils which form at the base, also from self-sown seed. The first bulbs reached Britain about a century ago by way of the Vienna Botanical Gardens. 4–6 inches.

H. dalmaticus. It is too rare and expensive to be grown by the hundred, but half a dozen bulbs planted in a bowl or in the pocket of

44. *Tulipa turkestanica*. From four to eight flowers are carried on a single stem. The open flowers are starlike, creamy white with rich brown stamens

45. *Tulipa Kaufmanniana*. 'The Water-Lily Tulip'

46. *Crocus medius.* Autumn flowering Crocus—lilac-purple blooms with orange stigmas

47. *Colchicum autumnale.* 'Meadow Saffron'

a rockery will prove a source of real pleasure with their Cambridge blue flower spikes. In a sheltered, sunny position it blooms during March, and if snow threatens, cover with a cloche. 4 inches.

IRIS

A number of the bulbous Irish species must be considered as amongst the most handsome subjects of the garden, yet it is surprising how few people grow them. Most are suitable for pot culture indoors and it is surprising that more are not commercially grown for sale in pots, when they would make a welcome change from the usual Tulips and Hyacinths. I am thinking particularly of *Iris reticulata*, which will come into bloom in January, reaching a height of eight to nine inches. This is the 'netted' iris, so called on account of the strange netted coating of the bulbs. It will prove an outstanding plant for a rockery, thanks to its dainty foliage and habit. The plants are at their best when planted near a rock, particularly if it is a piece of weathered Yorkshire stone, greyish white in colour, which shows off the rich purple, crimson and pale blue colours of the bloom to the greatest advantage. On the rockery or as an edging to a border it will come into bloom in mid-February, at a height of only six or seven inches. Planted in short grass where it looks delightful, it will reach a height of nine or ten inches. In the semi-shade of trees, particularly among silver birch, with their brightly coloured winter bark, the bulbs may be left untouched for several years, after which they are best lifted, divided and replanted during September. Plant the bulbs only two inches deep and two inches apart outdoors, for their habit is neat and upright and they make only a few rush-like leaves. Though they like a soil containing some peat or leaf mould and even a little decayed manure, lime rubble is, to all members of the Iris family, the most important part of their diet; and plenty of mortar should be worked into the soil beofre the bulbs are planted in autumn. A dressing with lime rubble each autumn will keep the bulbs healthy and free-flowering. When the blooms begin to die back, they should be removed, so as to conserve the energies of the plant as much as possible.

It is as pot plants that the Dwarf irises are at their best and the bulbs should be planted in pots or bowls in September. Plant them only an inch apart, and as many as a dozen bulbs may be planted in an earthenware bulb bowl. After two months in the plunge bed, or in a cool, dark place, they may be slowly introduced to the living-room. In early spring, their richly coloured blooms will scent a large room.

Species and varieties

I. Bakeriana. It is expensive, a single bulb costing 5*s.*, and so it may be advisable to grow it in small pots. From the first days of the year it sends up its exquisite violet-scented flowers on six-inch stems. The blooms are of such glorious shades of ultramarine, violet and blue as almost to defy description. Instead of trying, give up smoking for a week and plant two bulbs in a small pot.

I. Danfordiae. A light, well-drained soil containing plenty of lime rubble, and a sunny situation are all that it requires. Once established, do not disturb it for it is from the newly formed bulblets that next season's flowers will arise. It bears its golden-yellow flowers, speckled with brown, during February, and is almost leafless at flowering time. It blooms on a four-inch stem and is untroubled by the severest weather, for the flowers will emerge through frozen snow.

I. histrioides. As with all the Iris species, it is most important that, after flowering is over and the foliage has died down, the bulbs should be kept as dry as possible while they ripen through summer; so always select as dry and a sunny a position as possible; and if you grow them indoors, withhold moisture for several weeks after the bulbs have lost their foliage.

Coming into bloom in the open in early March, this is a charming little Iris to follow *I. Danfordiae,* and just as hardy. Its flowers of ultramarine crested with gold appear before the leaves and are larger and more brilliant than those of *I. reticulata.* 6 inches.

I. reticulata. It follows *I. histrioides* into bloom and is one of the more charming plants of garden and alpine house. Established plant increase rapidly and bloom year after year. The dark velvety-purple blooms have a vivid splash of orange on the fall petals and there are a number of varieties which are equally impressive. Possibly the most ouststanding is 'Cantab', so named because of the pure Cambridge blue colour of the blooms, accentuated by the orange stripe on the fall petals. It blooms on only six-inch stems while the others grow to a height of eight or nine inches. As a contrast to 'Cantab', 'Royal Blue' is of Oxford blue with a yellow blotch on the fall petals; 'Wentworth' is royal purple and, like those of 'Royal Blue', the flowers are large, the petals broad. Another excellent variety is 'J. S. Dijt', with reddish-purple flowers, and, as is the case with the others, it carries a strong violet perfume. 'Hercules' is of an unusual shade of bronzy-violet, and the new 'Harmony' has flowers of sky-blue with a bold yellow ridge on the fall petals.

Of all the Dwarf irises, *I. reticulata* is the one which most requires a sunny, well-drained situation if the bulbs are not to decay.

LEUCOJUM

Unfortunately, the 'Summer Snowflake' grows rather too tall to find a niche in this book on miniature bulbs, but the 'Spring Snowflake', *Leucojum vernum*, which grows only six inches tall, is one of the best of spring-flowering plants. The name *Leucojum* is derived from the Greek, meaning 'White Violet', though the flower more closely resembles a Snowdrop and enjoys much the same conditions (a moist but well-drained soil and a cool, shaded situation). It makes an ideal pot plant, coming into bloom six weeks before those growing in the open, when the blooms first appear in mid-March. The bulbs should be potted late in August to be placed beneath a wall and well covered with ashes. They are taken indoors in early December and should be kept reasonably dry. The blooms will remain fresh and fragrant for fully a month.

For outdoor flowering, plant three inches deep in September and the same distance apart, sprinkling a little peat over and below the bulbs to prevent excess moisture remaining about the bulbs.

Species

L. vernum. Its drooping bells are white, prettily tipped with bright yellow or green, the petals rounded and pleasingly fragrant. In bloom during March and April, the bulbs should be planted on the rockery or along the side of a path, or they may be massed in short grass. 6 inches.

LILIUM maculatum

This is the only Lily to be given a place in a book on miniature bulbs and it is quite outstanding in every way. It grows less than twelve inches high and may be planted in groups of three or four about a shrubbery or herbaceous border, and it is excellent for bedding. In 60-size pots in the alpine house or in a sunny window of the house, the plants will provide a pleasing display with their cup-shaped blooms held up to the light. The flowers often measure as much as six inches across when fully open, and they appear in clusters at the end of the main stems. As this Lily is stem-rooting, it should be planted five to six inches deep in a light loam, early in spring, placed on and covered with a mixture of peat and sand, so that surplus moisture may drain away from the bulbs.

Varieties

There are numerous varieties of *L. maculatum*, but outstanding is 'Kikat', with its blooms of deep apricot spotted with black, and borne on nine-inch stems. 'Alice Wilson', with lemon-yellow flowers, and the early-flowering *sanguineum* with crimson blooms spotted with black, are also most distinctive. Also striking is 'Mahogany', which has thick broad petals of deep crimson flushed with mahogany. The variety *bicolor* is also handsome, its brilliant orange flowers tipped and splashed with crimson.

MUSCARI

The Grape Hyacinths are seen at their best when planted amongst the miniature Hybrid daffodils, those which bloom at a height of from eight to twelve inches. Or plant them with *Juliae* primroses or with Gerard's old Double White primrose, or 'Cloth of Gold', a double yellow variety, for they are all in bloom at the same time. *Muscari botryoides album*, with its dainty white bells, is particularly well placed in a bed of dark red primroses. The bulbs are most inexpensive, costing, in many instances, only 2s. per dozen, so that they could well be planted with much greater lavishness and there are many species and hybrid varieties to choose from, quite apart from the well-known 'Heavenly Blue'; 8-cm. bulbs will give the best results, and these should be planted towards the end of September. After several years, the bulbs will have formed large clumps which should be lifted and divided, otherwise there will gradually be a reduction in quality and quantity of bloom. The most suitable time for lifting and dividing is in early summer, just before the foliage has died down. They may then be easily located. Before replanting, work into the soil any humus-forming material, together with a small quantity of fine shingle or coarse sand. *Muscari* enjoy a sunny position under a wall, but they are most tolerant of shade and even of adverse soil conditions.

To those who enjoy a scented flower, I would recommend the tiny species, *moschatum flavum*, which still has the true musk perfume, and from which the *Muscari* originally took its name. This romantic little plant should be set in a seed pan containing loam, peat, sand and some gravel chippings in September, and should be brought into the house after Christmas. Plant a dozen bulbs to a pan, and what a treat you will have! Late in February, provided the bulbs are in no way forced, they will send up five-inch spikes of purple and yellow with the most magnificent perfume. Be careful not to give too much water, as this precious little flower comes from the dry region of Asia Minor. Or plant a dozen bulbs under the wall of the house, near to the entrance door, and their delicious scent will permeate the whole house on a warm, still day in early April. Set with them a few bulbs of the 'Hoop Petticoat' Daffodil, the lemon-yellow *Narcissus bulbocodium citrinus* (if you can obtain it) or a few plants of the fragrant woodland-perfumed *Polyanthus*, 'Barrowby Gem', with its heads of the sharp lemon yellow. Should the weather be poor take a spray of each indoors, and there drink of their fragrance to the full.

Species and hybrid varieties

M. argaei album. This is a distinctive plant which blooms during May and June, producing tiny spikes of chalk white which last for many weeks. 4 inches.

M. armeniacum 'Cantab'. This is one of the loveliest of all the *Muscari*, its sturdy spikes of a good shade of Cambridge blue produced with freedom. It makes a pleasing contrast with the cobalt-blue spires of 'Blue Pearl'. 6 inches.

M. botryoides. This is the 'Italian' Grape Hyacinth, its tightly packed spikes of dark blue globular flowers resembling a bunch of black grapes. It flowers throughout April and into May and to see it at its best, plant with it the white form, *album*. 6 inches.

M. comosum. Described by Louise Wilder as a 'quaint monstrosity', the 'Tassel Hyacinth' grows a foot high, taller than most. The spike, produced during April and May, descends from top to bottom in shades of brown to green and blue, and it is excellent for indoor decoration. It has a pleasing fragrance.

M. conicum 'Heavenly Blue'. This is possibly the best-known of all the *Muscari*. It is the 'Starch Hyacinth' and bears many conical spikes of gentian-blue, agreeably scented. The tiny globular bells are packed tightly together on nine-inch stems, making this an excellent form for planting in grass and for cutting. It is in its prime during April.

M. latifolium. Has broad, strap-like leaves like those of the Arum lily, from which the dark blue bud pushes up to open pale blue at the top, dark blue at the base. An interesting and free-flowering species for April. 10 inches.

M. moschatum flavum. The bloom of the 'Musk Hyacinth', from which the whole family takes its name, is anything but beautiful, the purple 'grapes' turning first grey and then to an uninteresting shade of browny-yellow. The perfume, however, is pungent and incense-like, a few blooms scenting a large room. Plant it in those odd corners about the garden where it may be left undisturbed to distil its fragrance during March and April. 6 inches.

M. neglectum. This is a most attractive little chap, with blue-black spikes on short sturdy stems above greenish-yellow foliage. It is free flowering and blooms through April and May. 6 inches.

M. paradoxum. The bulbs are cheap enough, and the blooms quite beautiful, large and of a unique shade of peacock-green. The foliage is neat and tidy, so this is an excellent species for the rockery, at its best during April. 6 inches.

M. plumosum. This is the 'Feather Hyacinth'. Its blooms are sterile, and drawn out like fine threads, so that it has a feather-like appearance. Its rich violet 'feathers' are borne in May and are most useful for 'mixing' with other miniature flowers for indoor decoration. 9 inches.

M. polyanthum album. A native of Greece with, in April and May, dainty spikes of rich creamy white flowers which are in delightful contrast to the blue-flowered forms. 6 inches.

M. Tubergenianum. Known as the 'Oxford and Cambridge Hyacinth' and was introduced from Northern Persia during recent years. The top half of the bloom is of Cambridge blue, the lower portion of Oxford blue without any trace of purple colouring. The large blooms are borne from the end of April until well into June and are excellent for cutting. 9 inches.

NARCISSUS

The fairy-like Miniature narcissus species are extremely hardy and long lasting, the tiny blooms nodding in the spring breezes quite equal to withstanding wintry conditions. For the rockery, for planting around the roots of young trees, as an edging to a path, for a trough garden or window box, and for indoor culture in pots, the little Daffodils should be more frequently planted. They are easily grown in any ordinary fibrous loam to which a little peat has been added. Small pockets should be prepared on the rockery to take four or five bulbs, planted early in September after the rockery has been thoroughly cleaned and the established plants stripped of any straggling growth. For a window box or tub it is not always convenient to plant before mid-October, which will not be too late, as the miniatures do not seem to require so long a season in which to make root growth. They may, however, take eighteen months to come into bloom, but then will bloom most prolifically and will rapidly increase, from bulblets, to form large clumps. They should be left untouched for as long as possible and only when they begin to show less bloom should they be lifted and divided. This is best done after flowering and before the foliage dies down, in the same way that Snowdrops are divided. The foliage should not, of course, be removed until it has finally turned brown and died back.

Species and varieties

N. bulbocodium. The 'Hoop Petticoat' Daffodil and a charming little plant which likes a sunny position and a light, sandy soil but one containing peat or leaf mould to retain moisture. The tiny yellow trumpets, borne amidst rush-like foliage, are backed by star-like petals of pale yellow. The form, *citrinus* has flowers of pale citron-yellow; *conspicuus* is bright golden-yellow. It will take fully a year to become established and will bloom in March on six-inch stems. The form *Romieuxii* is the earliest of all to bloom, for it will bear its sulphur-yellow flowers during February if given a sunny, sheltered position.

N. canaliculatus. This little Polyanthus Narcissus bears three or four sweetly scented flowers to each stem, their tiny golden cups enhanced by a pure white perianth. The narrow, erect, greenish-blue foliage is also beautiful. It blooms during April and will appreciate the shelter of a sunny rockery. 6 inches.

N. capax plenus. This is 'Queen Anne's Double Daffodil' with six rows of lemon-yellow petals so arranged as to give the bloom a star-like symmetry.

N. cernuus. This is the old 'Nodding Daffodil' which comes early

167

into bloom and bears silvery-white nodding flowers above blue-green foliage. 9 inches.

N. cyclamineus. The 'Cyclamen-flowered' Daffodil, so called because of its reflexed perianth. It is one of the first Daffodils to bloom and is at its best by the side of a stream, for it likes a peaty, moist soil and the protection of grass in summer. The most interesting variety is one of recent introduction called 'Snipe', which grows to a height of nine inches and makes a delightful pot plant. The reflexed perianth is of pure white, the trumpet deep yellow. Another good new variety is 'Peeping Tom', with long, elegant golden-yellow trumpet and a perianth of the same colour. Even more compact is 'Beryl', which has a tiny globular orange cup and a reflexed perianth of primrose-yellow. 9 inches.

N. gracilis. It blooms early in June and is the latest of all the Daffodils to flower, but well worth waiting for. Its blooms carry the strongest perfume of all the numerous bulbous plants. Four or five pale yellow blooms appear on each twelve-inch stem and their fragrance is carried far from the plants.

N. 'Hawera'. It is a *N. triandrus* hybrid of robust habit and bearing, to each stem three or four canary-yellow blooms with dainty reflexed perianths. 8 inches.

N. juncifolius. The 'Rush-leaf Daffodil' of the Pyrenees, in bloom in April. It is quite happy in the shelter of rockery stones and is charming in pans in the alpine house, but does not like open ground planting. Is highly scented, with a unique large trumpet. An additional virtue is that after flowering its leaves die back almost out of sight. 4 inches.

N. lobularis. With *N. cyclamineus* and *N. minimus*, it is among the earliest to bloom, the first buds showing colour by March 1st. It is extremely dainty, with a primrose-yellow trumpet and sulphur perianth. 8 inches.

N. minimus. This is the smallest of all the trumpet daffodils, bearing its dainty fringed trumpets on stems of only four inches. Though useful along the edge of a path or border, this fairy-like daffodil is at its best in pans in the alpine house. Outdoors it enjoys a sunny situation and a peaty soil, well drained. It comes into bloom in March with *N. cyclamineus.*

M. nanus. Useful in that it follows *N. lobularis*, in bloom during March, and so keeps continuity from February to May with these dainty rock-garden species. It bears an exquisite yellow

48. Scarcely taller than a matchbox and tinted in various colours, these crocus glasses may be used for growing Scillas, Grape Hyacinths, miniature Narcissi, etc., besides the various crocus species

49. Bulbs in glasses should be placed in a cool dark place until a good root system is formed. The picture shows the stage at which they should be brought into the light. Bulbs grown in this way should always be kept in a cool position

50. Known as *Acorn Glasses* these miniature glasses may be used to grow the smaller bulbs, such as Snowdrops, and the smaller species of Crocus and Muscari

51. Miniature tulip species are happy planted five bulbs in a five-inch plant pot

52. Bulbs of 'Glory of the Snow'. Left: *Chionodoxa sardensis*; Right: *Chionodoxa luciliae*

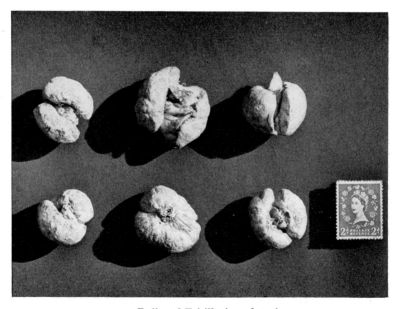

53. Bulbs of *Fritillaria meleagris*

54. Bulbs of *Allium moly*, 'The Golden Garlic

55. Bulbs of *Iris reticulata*

56. The curiously shaped tubers of *Iris tuberosa*

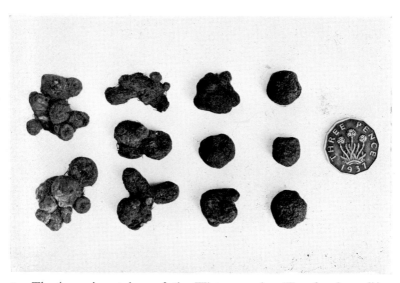

57. The 'corms' or tubers of the Winter aconite (*Eranthus hyemalis*) though smaller, resemble those of Anemones. These plants belong to the same family

58. The corms of *Crocus ancyrensis* have beautifully reticulated tunics

59. Corms of Freesia

60. Planting bulbs of Iris reticulata

61. Planting bulbs of *Fritillaria mele-agris*

62. Planting corms of miniature Crocus species. Twelve in a six-inch seed-pan

63. Pans of miniature bulbs provide colour in the alpine house or cold greenhouse from January onwards

64. Pans of *Crocus chrysanthus* brought indoors and placed on a window ledge soon fill a room with delicious fragrance (in February)

bloom, the exact replica of a 'King Alfred Daffodil', on six-inch stems.

N. odorus. The Spanish campernelle, highly scented. It should be planted at the edge of a border beneath a window to allow its fragrance to enter the house during May. The star-like blooms are borne in clusters of three or four on eight-inch stems. There is also an attractive double form known as 'Queen Anne's Irish Jonquil', of a warm gold colour and deliciously scented.

N. 'Rip van Winkle' reached this country from Ireland and is a Double Daffodil with narrow, twisted petals of pale yellow, deepening in colour at the centre, and tinted with green. It blooms in March on a six-inch stem and is one of the most exquisite of all the miniature daffodils.

N. rupicola. Where left undisturbed it will seed itself profusely, the bright yellow flowers having a six-sided corona and the same rush-like leaves as *N. juncifolius*, to which it is allied, both being found together in the Pyrenees. 4 inches.

N. tenuior. It is to be found along the shores of the Mediterranean and is known as the 'Silver Jonquil'. It comes late into bloom and is at its best at the end of May and early in June. Three or four blooms, richly perfumed, appear on each stem, with sulphur-yellow cup and a perianth of silvery cream. 8 inches.

N. triandrus albus. The 'Angel's Tears Daffodil' which was discovered by the late Mr. Peter Barr on the borders of Portugal and Spain. It produces a cluster of tiny creamy-white flowers of globular cup and reflexed perianth which droop gracefully like Snowdrops, and give the impression of tear drops. Blooms on six-inch stems during April.

N. Watieri. It comes from the Atlas Mountains of Morocco and is a delicately-formed species, though quite hardy in a sunny position and in a well-drained soil, its blooms pure white and circular in form, on four-inch stems. It is in flower in May.

N. 'Wee Bee'. A tiny hybrid after the style of *N. minimus* and bearing golden-yellow flowers of perfect form on four-inch stems.

N. 'W. P. Milner'. It is almost too tall to be classed as a miniature for it surmounts a twelve-inch stem, but is quite outstanding. Pure white, it comes early into bloom.

ORNITHOGALUM

The 'Star of Bethlehem' which blooms during May and June. It will flourish almost anywhere, in short grass beneath tall trees and where the grass does not require cutting; or about a shrubbery, where the ground is not disturbed and where the display may be expected to increase each year by means of bulblets and self-sown seed. The bulbs should be planted three inches deep in October into soil containing some peat or leaf mould. Grit or coarse sand should be incorporated if the soil is heavy.

Species

O. Balansae. A dwarf species from Asia Minor, with large umbels of glistening white flowers which appear before the end of May on six-inch stems.

O. nutans. A native of the woodlands of Southern Europe, it bears graceful spikes of blooms of a lovely shade of silvery-grey, shaded on the outside with pale green, during early summer. The spikes are excellent for cutting, being long lasting both when in water and when left growing in the open. 8 inches.

O. umbellatum. This is the true 'Star of Bethlehem' and may be gathered on the hills around that ancient city. In the Middle East the bulbs are roasted and eaten. Its white flowers are borne in loose umbels of eight or nine blooms on six-inch stems, and appear during May and June.

OXALIS

Most of us know only too well the pink *Oxalis floribunda* of cottage gardens, popularly called 'Wood Sorrel'. *O. acetellosa* is our shade-loving native Wood Sorrel. It will sow its own seed rather too freely and often becomes more of a nuisance than a pleasure. But several species have much to commend them. They have a flowering season extending from May until mid-November and are of the utmost value on the rockery and in a sunny position in the shrubbery, even under woodland trees. Although not averse to sun, they enjoy best a cool, leafy soil, fairly moist but by no means waterlogged. If sufficient leaf mould is not present, work in quantities of peat or rotted manure. September is the right time for planting the tubers only just beneath the soil surface. The dainty November-flowering *Oxalis variabilis*, also a most suitable plant for the rockery, should be planted in April. All *Oxalis* will enjoy a liberal mulching with peat or leaf mould during October.

Species

O. adenophylla. So inexpensive to buy and yet so rarely seen. From South America, and bearing its rosy-pink flowers on but two-inch stalks throughout early summer, this species appreciates some limestone in the soil and seems also to like a leafy soil, but one that is not acid.

O. Bowieana. Like a Rock-rose in form and bearing its bright rose flowers with golden centres throughout June and July. Found in its natural state on Table Mountain, South Africa, and so it must be given a warm, sunny position and a soil containing plenty of grit. 9 inches.

O. braziliensis. From Brazil, and so requires a warm pocket in the rockery where it will receive full sunshine and some slight protection. Bears most arresting little blooms of deep wine red. I have this growing with several plants of *Ramonda nathaliae*, which has bright lavender-blue flowers. The combination is particularly delightful throughout June. 4 inches.

O. Deppei. From Mexico, and the exception to the rule of shallow planting. The tubers should be planted in beds of almost complete leaf mould six inches deep. Has flowers of an unusual brick red colour from June until late August. The foliage is also of a captivating green and purple colouring. There is a white-flowered form of equal beauty. The roots are delicious when cooked. 6 inches.

O. enneaphylla. A native of the Falkland Isles and a superb plant, the large waxy white cup-shaped blooms having a distinct green centre. In flower throughout the summer. 3 inches.

O. lobata. Losing its leaves in June, when it should be divided, this *Oxalis* produces masses of golden-yellow flowers in the manner of a Colchicum in September. It needs the same treatment as *O. Bowieana*. 4 inches.

PUSCHKINIA

The 'Lebanon Squill' blooms throughout spring and enjoys a position where sunshine may penetrate and a well-drained soil, for an excess of winter moisture will cause the bulbs to decay. Work in plenty of grit and coarse sand in addition to some peat or leaf mould, and plant the bulbs four inches deep in October. They may be planted about a rockery, in the alpine house or beneath trees where the grass has died back and will not need cutting. But for the plants to be a success it is necessary for the bulbs to be exposed to summer sunshine and become well ripened.

Native of the hilly country stretching from Afghanistan to the Lebanon, the individual blooms are so good to look at that they should be enjoyed at close quarters, and so they are at their best in the trough garden or window box, or in small pots indoors. A raised rockery will also show them to full advantage. Extremely easy to grow, the bulbs cost very little and should be freely planted.

Species

P. scilloides. Known as the 'Lebanon' or 'Striped' Squill, its blooms of palest sky-blue, are striped with porcelain-blue down the centre and at the sides of each petal. Several blooms, which measure half an inch in diameter when fully open, are borne on each stem above upright leaves of rich, glossy green. 6 inches.

RANUNCULUS aconitifolius

As distinct from the French and Persian hybrids, which are valuable for bedding and cut flower purposes, the uncommon 'White Buttercup' of Central Europe, *R. aconitifolius*, is a valuable plant for planting in low-lying ground, as it is able to tolerate any amount of moisture. During May and June it bears masses of creamy-white buttercups with attractively 'cut' foliage, like that of the Monkshood. The flowers are in sprays of ten to twelve inches and are valuable for cutting. There is a beautiful double form known as 'Fair Maids of France', but it is rather taller growing.

RHODOHYPOXIS. See Chapter 11.

ROMULEA. See Chapter 11.

SCILLA

Both the English Blue-bell with its arching sprays of violet-blue bells and the Spanish Hyacinth with its tightly packed spikes of bells, grow rather too tall for our present purposes. The true Squills, which bloom several weeks earlier and grow to no more than six inches, are, however, quite delightful plants and may be planted about a rockery or massed beneath trees. To the front of a shrubbery they are equally charming, their dainty sprays appearing from between two bronzy-green leaves. They are in flower at the same time as the Snowdrops and should be planted with them, for the clear China blue of the Squills provides a delightful contrast to the snow-white of the Snow-drops. In short grass, beneath trees, the plants will receive the early spring sunshine and the bulbs will remain cool during summer when the trees are in full leaf. The blue-flowered Scillas should be planted round the foot of silver birches.

The Scillas like a soil with plenty of leaf mould; yet, contrary to popular belief, they are never happy in an acid soil. The soil of a town garden should be given a dressing of lime before the bulbs are planted two to three inches deep, and the same distance apart, in October.

The Scillas are delightful plants for the alpine house, or for a cool room. Like the Snowdrops and other early-flowering bulbs of extreme hardiness, they should be grown cold throughout and should not be taken indoors until the New Year, after they have been ten weeks in the plunge bed. The best species for pot culture is *S. Tubergeniana*, for each bulb will bear four flower spikes, each having up to a dozen blooms.

Species and varieties

S. amethystina. It should not be confused with *Hyacinthus amethystinus* for it blooms during May and June, and is thus extremely valuable for extending the display to give six months of colour from the Miniature squills. A native of Dalmatia, it produces pyramidal spikes of clear porcelain-blue. Do not plant it in grass which requires cutting during summer, but in the shrubbery or rockery. 8 inches.

S. bifolia. A native of Asia Minor, it blooms during February and March, sending up its sprays of gentian-blue between two bronzy-green leaves from dense clumps. The six-petalled blooms dangle and dance in the spring breezes but are happiest in a sheltered position. The form *rosea* bears flowers which are of a good shade of soft shell-pink. Where undisturbed, the plants seed freely. 6 inches.

S. pratensis. It is inexpensive and lovely, coming into bloom early in May, with flowers of deepest blue on six- to eight-inch stems. Of neat, compact habit, it is excellent for alpine lawn and rockery.

S. sibirica. A native of the Northern shores of Russia and one of the hardiest of all bulbs. It is also one of the most free-flowering, bearing spikes of electric-blue flowers in rapid succession from late February until well into April. There is a pure white form, *alba*, and the new hybrid, 'Spring Beauty', has spikes of rich purple-blue which are twice the size of the species and borne with great freedom, so that it is an ideal window-box plant. The spikes of *S. sibirica* attain a height of four inches, those of 'Spring Beauty' eight inches.

S. Tubergeniana. The bulbs cost a shilling each and so should be treated with respect; but without any doubt, this is one of the choicest of all the miniature bulbs. Each bulb will produce four or more spikes which are densely packed with as many as a dozen blooms of a rich China blue with a deep turquoise stripe down each petal. The flower spikes come just before the leaves, and the blooms are seen to best advantage on the rockery, planted close to the snowdrops or the white-flowered *S. sibirica alba.* Or plant three bulbs to a 2½-inch pot to enjoy a succession of flower spikes throughout February. 5 inches.

S. verna. It is native to Britain and bears its racemes of Cambridge blue flowers throughout April. The very large flowers are often more than half an inch in diameter, and when cut will remain fresh in water for a considerable time. 4 inches.

SPARAXIS. See Chapter 11.

STERNBERGIA

The 'Lily of the Field' of Biblical times, and what a lovely little crocus-like plant this is, with shining lemon yellow flowers all the better for a dry, sunny position. We have the Dog's Tooth Violet for shade, the Scilla and Snowdrop for partial shade, and the Sternbergia is of the utmost value for a dry corner in full sun. The drier the site and the hotter the sun, the more lavishly it produces its rich yellow blooms. It does take a little time to get established and should never be lifted except when growing in a clay soil, for it will increase but slowly. It is almost completely hardy, but in an exposed garden the bulbs should be planted four to five inches deep and given a light peat mulch during November. As it is necessary for the continued vigour of the bulbs that they become thoroughly ripened before growth begins again the following year, it will be necessary to lift the bulbs every November where they are growing in a cold, heavy soil. They should be carefully cleaned and dried in a warm greenhouse or roof, and replanted the following spring.

Species

S. Fischeriana. Also from the Middle East and bears its dainty golden-yellow flowers throughout February. This species should be planted in September when *lutea* is in bloom.

S. lutea. Also known as the 'Yellow Star Flower'. It is found wild in Israel, growing in arid rocky country, and those are the conditions it best enjoys in Britain. It flowers during early autumn. Its glossy strap-like leaves do not appear until late in spring and die back after flowering. The secret of success with this plant is to grow it as dry as possible. Plant early in spring before its leaves appear. 8 inches.

STREPTANTHERA. See Chapter 11.

TECOPHILAEA. See Chapter 11.

TRILLIUM

The 'American Wood Lilies' are happiest in shade and in a moist soil, containing leaf mould. *T. cernuum* grows twelve inches tall and bears drooping white flowers during April and May above large decorative leaves. *T. grandiflorum* grows to a similar height. It is known as the 'Snow Trillium' and has large, three-petalled flowers of pure white and glossy green leaves. These are delightful in the woodland garden.

TRITONIA. See Chapter 11.

TULIP

Among bulbous plants, the Tulip species stand supreme for the richness of their oriental colourings; their blooms have a clarity and intensity of colour to be found in no other plants. Yet whereas the Dutch hybrids are grown in their millions for bedding display, and are often used for no more than a single season, the numerous charming species may be naturalised in short grass, planted about the shrubbery or rockery, and used for trough garden or window-box display; and, what is more, they are just as long lasting as all the other miniature bulbs. There are a number of Tulip species which, because of their tall habit, are most suitable for planting in long grass, but they can find no place in this book, useful as they might be. There are many species of dwarf habit which are so diverse in character that they should be planted as freely as possible to provide colour and interest from early March until the end of May. Most of them like an open, sunny situation and a well-drained sandy soil which will permit the bulbs to become thoroughly ripe after flowering. This is important if they are to be long-living and free-flowering. The bulbs may be planted out up to the end of November, set three to four inches deep and the same distance apart. They will produce a more brilliant display if planted in groups of three.

Species and varieties

T. australis. Produces its yellow, red-flushed, star-shaped blooms on six-inch stems. When in the bud stage they nod in the wind like Snowdrops. At their best throughout April.

T. Batalini. This is a most beautiful species for the alpine garden, producing in April dainty flowers of soft creamy-yellow with bright golden centres. It rarely exceeds four inches in height, and its leaves trail on the ground.

T. biflora. It is a dainty species from the Caucasus, having narrow leaves and bearing from the main stems two to four starry creamy-white blooms shaded green on the exterior. 5 inches.

T. chrysantha. This little pet from the Himalayas is in bloom during May, the blooms rich yellow on the inside, shaded cherry-red on the outside. 8 inches.

T. dasystemon. A gem for the rock garden, bearing several flowers on each stem of palest yellow, shaded green and grey on the outside. It is April flowering and grows only six inches tall.

T. Eichleri. This is a brilliant April-flowering Tulip for bedding or naturalising, with large scarlet bloom whose black centre is surrounded with a golden band. It grows ten inches high and comes from Southern Russia.

T. Fosteriana 'Princeps'. It grows only eight inches tall and is the only member of the group sufficiently dwarf for inclusion in this book. The large scarlet blooms have a black and yellow centre and are at their best during April.

T. Greigii. The blooms are the largest of all Tulips and are of glowing orange, blotched with maroon at the centre. The foliage, too, is spotted with maroon. April flowering. 9 inches.

T. Hageri. This is a most beautiful Tulip from Greece, with small, globular blooms of dull coppery-red shaded with olive green outside. It is in bloom during April. 9 inches.

T. Kaufmanniana. Native of the hilly regions of Central Asia, it is known as the 'Water Lily Tulip' on account of the shape of the blooms when open. The petals are broad and the flowers open to an enormous size. They are the first of all the Tulips to bloom, showing colour by mid-March. There are a number of excellent new varieties and hybrids of which 'Gaiety' is outstanding, the deep cream blooms, striped red on the outside almost resting on the leaves.

Another gem is 'Scarlet Elegance', the vivid scarlet flowers with golden base, held on six-inch stems. Growing to a similar height is 'Shakespeare', the flowers an exquisite blending of apricot, salmon and orange. Extremely showy is 'Elliott', of white blooms with red markings on the outside, and most striking of all is the new hybrid 'Robert Schumann', the latest to bloom, its flowers of chrome-yellow flushed with rose on the exterior, the centre splashed with black blotches.

T. Kolpakowskiana. This is a splendid Tulip from Asia Minor flowering in April; its deep golden-yellow flowers, unusually long, shaded with rose on the exterior, are held on nine-inch stems.

T. linifolia. It bears during May, its tiny blooms of glowing scarlet with blue centre, on six-inch stems. Glaucous foliage.

T. Maximowicizii. Though under six inches, it has large flowers of shining deep scarlet, the petals having a dark blotch at the base. In flower during April.

T. persica. The 'Persian Tulip', charming for a trough garden or rockery. Fragrant blooms in May of deep yellow, shaded with bronze on the outside. Grows only three inches high.

T. primulina. Two or more flowers are produced from each bulb and are white, flushed with green and margined with rose. The glaucous foliage adds to its beauty. It grows nine inches tall and blooms during April.

T. pulchella. It comes into bloom at the end of March, its long urn-shaped blooms, of a lovely shade of soft mauve with a pale yellow centre, opening flat in the sun. 4 inches.

T. saxatilis. It must have a dry, warm position and a soil containing plenty of grit and sand, and the bulbs should be planted deeply. The delightful silvery lavender flowers are produced throughout May, and its broad glossy green foliage, unique in the genus, adds to its charm. 9 inches.

T. Tubergeniana. This is a most striking Tulip which grows ten inches high, its handsome scarlet flowers, with black blotches at the base, opening as wide as the flower grows tall. It blooms during May.

T. turkestanica. It is of similar habit to *T. biflora* in that three or four blooms appear from the main stem. It is one of the earliest to bloom. The cream-coloured flowers, attractively flushed with green and rose on the exterior, are borne on six-inch stems during March.

T. Wilsoniana. From Persia, and also called *T. montana.* It forms long, narrow leaves and bears large cups of cherry-red which almost sit on the soil. It blooms late, in May. 3 inches.

ZEPHYRANTHES

Known as the 'Zephyr Flower' or 'Flower of the West Wind', these flowers are as attractive as their names. Natives of Peru, the bulbs are believed to be somewhat tender, but in a sandy, well-drained soil will prove hardy in most gardens. This, however, does not mean that the plants prefer a dry position, for the bulbs enjoy plenty of moisture during summer and when in bloom in autumn. Plant the bulbs three inches deep on a layer of peat. Those species that bloom in autumn should be planted in April. The exception is *Z. atamasco*, which blooms in May and should be planted in September. Where established, the bulbs should be left undisturbed for years, since they will increase both from offsets and from self-sown seed. The plants require an open, sunny position and are never happy in shade, so plant to the front of a shrubbery or in grass which should not be cut until the early spring, by which time the foliage will have died back. The plants will appreciate it if the grass in which they grow is dressed with peat after it has been cut.

Species

Z. Andersonii. Of dwarf habit, it makes an excellent alpine garden plant and bears its shining orange blooms throughout August. 5 inches.

Z. atamasco. Also known as *Z. rosea* it is one of the two species to bloom in summer, being at its best during May and early June. Its handsome white Crocus-like flowers are striped and tinted with rosy-lilac, and its glossy green leaves appear with the flowers. 7 inches.

Z. candida. This is perhaps the most beautiful of all the Zephyranthes, producing during autumn a profusion of pure white Crocus-like flowers amid a mass of rush-like leaves. The whiteness of the petals is enhanced by the gold of the stamens. 8 inches.

Z. carinata. A native of the West Indies and not quite so hardy as the others, so must be given some winter protection. This is one of the few small flowering species to bloom in July, when it produces its delicately coloured shell-pink blooms on six-inch stems.

HARDY BULBS

Species	Flowering Time	Planting Time	Height
Allium anceps	August	October	6 ins.
,, *cyaneum*	July–Aug.	October	4 ins.
,, *karataviense*	May	Sept.–Oct.	10 ins.
,, *moly*	June	October	12 ins.
,, *ostrowskianum*	May–June	October	6 ins.
Anemone apennina	March–April	April and October	6 ins.
,, *blanda*	March–April	September	3 ins.
,, *fulgens*	April–June	October	12 ins.
,, *nemorosa*	April–June	September	6 ins.
,, *palmata*	May–June	September	8 ins.
,, *ranunculoides*	April–June	September	4 ins.
Brodiaea coccinea	June–July	September	12 ins.
,, *crocea*	May–June	September	6 ins.
,, *grandiflora*	June	September	8 ins.
,, *ixioides*	June	September	9 ins.
,, *minor*	June	September	6 ins.
,, *multiflora*	June–July	September	9 ins.
Bulbocodium vernum	March	Sept.–Oct.	3 ins.
Chionodoxa gigantea	April	September	5 ins.
,, *luciliae*	March–April	September	4 ins.
,, *sardensis*	March	September	4 ins.
,, *tmoli*	April	October	4 ins.
Colchicum agrippinum	Sept.–Oct.	July	4 ins.
,, *alpinum*	Aug.–Sept.	July	3 ins.
,, *autumnale*	Oct.–Nov.	July	6 ins.

Species		Flowering Time	Planting Time	Height
Colchicum	*Bornmuelleri*	Aug.–Sept.	July	8 ins.
„	*byzantinum*	Aug.–Oct.	July	6 ins.
„	*callicybium*	Sept.–Oct.	July	6 ins.
„	*luteum*	April	September	3 ins.
„	*speciosum*	Aug.–Nov.	July	9 ins.
Corydalis	*angustifolia*	March–May	October	8 ins.
„	*bulbosa*	April–May	October	4 ins.
„	*cava*	April–May	October	8 ins.
„	*decipiens*	May	October	9 ins.
„	*densiflora*	March–April	October	6 ins.
„	*Wilsonii*	April–May	October	8 ins.
Crocus	*ancyrensis*	Feb.–March	October	2 ins.
„	*asturicus*	Oct.–Nov.	July	3 ins.
„	*balansae*	March	October	1½ ins.
„	*biflorus*	March	October	3 ins.
„	*Boryi*	Nov.–Dec.	July	3 ins.
„	*cancellatus*	Oct.–Nov.	July	3 ins.
„	*candidus*	April	October	2 ins.
„	*chrysanthus*	Feb.–April	October	4 ins.
„	*corsicus*	March	October	3 ins.
„	*Fleischeri*	Feb.–April	October	2 ins.
„	*imperati*	Jan.–March	July	3 ins.
„	*Karduchorum*	Sept.–Oct.	July	4 ins.
„	*Kasmiriana*	October	July	3 ins.
„	*Korolkowi*	Jan.–March	September	1½ ins.
„	*laevigatus*	Dec.-Feb.	July	3 ins.
„	*longiflorus*	Nov.–Dec.	July	4 ins.
„	*medius*	October	July	3 ins.
„	*minimus*	March–April	October	1½ ins.
„	*niveus*	Dec.–March	July	4 ins.
„	*nudiflorus*	October	July	3 ins.
„	*ochroleucus*	Nov.–Dec.	July	2 ins.
„	*Olivieri*	April–May	October	2 ins.
„	*pulchellus*	Oct.–Nov.	July	3 ins.
„	*Salzmanni*	November	July	3 ins.
„	*sativus*	October	July	2 ins.
„	*Sieberi*	Feb.–March	October	3 ins.
„	*speciosus*	Sept.–Nov.	July	4 ins.

MINIATURE BULBS: ALPHABETICAL LIST

Species	Flowering Time	Planting Time	Height
Crocus susianus	March–April	October	3 ins.
„ *Tomasinianus*	Feb.–March	October	3 ins.
„ *Tournefortii*	November	July	3 ins.
„ *vernus*	March	October	2 ins.
„ *versicolor*	March	October	3 ins.
„ *zonatus*	Sept.–Oct.	July	3 ins.
Cyclamen africanum	Sept.–Nov.	June	4 ins.
„ *alpinum*	Dec.–Feb.	July	3 ins.
„ *Atkinsii*	Dec.–March	July	4 ins.
„ *cilicium*	Sept.–Nov.	March	3 ins.
„ *coum*	Jan.–April	July	3 ins.
„ *europaeum*	July–Aug.	March	4 ins.
„ *graceum*	July–Sept.	March	4 ins.
„ *libanoticum*	March–April	July	6 ins.
„ *neapolitanum*	Sept.–Nov.	March	4 ins.
„ *repandum*	April–May	July	6 ins.
Eranthis cilicica	Feb.–March	September	2 ins.
„ *hyemalis*	Jan.–Feb.	September	2 ins.
Erythronium californicum	March–April	September	12 ins.
„ *dens canis*	March–April	September	6 ins.
„ *Hendersonii*	April	September	4 ins.
„ *revolutum*	March	September	9 ins.
„ *tuolumnense*	March	September	12 ins.
Fritillaria citrina	April–May	September	6 ins.
„ *meleagris*	April–May	September	12 ins.
„ *pudica*	April–May	September	4 ins.
Galanthus Allenii	April	Sep. & Mar.	4 ins.
„ *byzantinus*	Dec.–Jan.	Sep. & Mar.	4 ins.
„ *'Colesbourne'*	Feb.–March	Sep. & Mar.	4 ins.
„ *Elwesii*	March	Sep. & Mar.	9 ins.
„ *imperati*	Dec.–Jan.	Sep. & Mar.	6 ins.
„ *latifolius*	March–April	Sep. & April	3 ins.
„ *nivalis*	Feb.–March	Sep. & April	5 ins.
„ *Olgae*	Oct.–Nov.	July	6 ins.
„ *plicatus*	March	Sep. & Mar.	8 ins.
Hyacinthus amethystinus	March–April	October	8 ins.
„ *azureus*	April	October	5 ins.
„ *dalmaticus*	April	October	4 ins.

MINIATURE BULBS: ALPHABETICAL LIST

Species	Flowering Time	Planting Time	Height
Iris Bakeriana	Jan.–Feb.	September	6 ins.
„ Danfordiae	February	September	4 ins.
„ histroides	March	September	6 ins.
„ reticulata	March–April	September	6 ins.
Leucojum vernum	March–April	September	6 ins.
Lilium maculatum	June–July	March	10 ins.
Muscari argaei album	May–June	October	4 ins.
„ armeniacum	April–May	September	6 ins.
„ botryoides	April–May	September	6 ins.
„ comosum	April–May	September	12 ins.
„ conicum	April	September	8 ins.
„ latifolium	April	September	10 ins.
„ moschatum flavum	March–April	September	6 ins.
„ neglectum	April–May	October	6 ins.
„ paradoxum	April	September	6 ins.
„ plumosum	May	October	9 ins.
„ polyanthum album	April–May	September	6 ins.
„ Tubergenianum	April–June	September	9 ins.
Narcissus bulbocodium	March–April	September	6 ins.
„ capax plenus	April	September	6 ins.
„ cernus	April	September	9 ins.
„ canaliculatus	April	September	6 ins.
„ cyclamineus	March	September	9 ins.
„ gracilis	May–June	September	12 ins.
„ juncifolius	April	September	4 ins.
„ lobularis	Feb.–March	September	8 ins.
„ minimus	Feb.–March	September	4 ins.
„ nanus	March–April	September	6 ins.
„ odorus	May	September	8 ins.
„ Rip van Winkle	March	September	6 ins.
„ rupicola	April	September	4 ins.
„ tenuior	May–June	September	9 ins.
„ triandrus	April	September	6 ins.
„ Watieri	May	September	4 ins.
„ 'Wee Bee'	April	September	4 ins.
Ornithogalum Balansae	May–June	October	6 ins.
„ nutans	May–June	October	8 ins.
„ umbellatum	May–June	October	6 ins.

Species	Flowering Time	Planting Time	Height
Oxalis adenophylla	May–June	September	3 ins.
„ *Bowieana*	June–July	September	9 ins.
„ *braziliensis*	June–July	September	4 ins.
„ *Deppei*	June–Aug.	September	6 ins.
„ *ennaphylla*	June–Aug.	September	3 ins.
„ *lobata*	September	June	4 ins.
Puschkinia scilloides	March–May	October	4 ins.
Ranunculus aconitifolius	May–June	October	10 ins.
Scilla amethystina	May–June	October	8 ins.
„ *bifolia*	Feb.-March	September	6 ins.
„ *pratensis*	May–June	October	7 ins.
„ *sibirica*	Feb.–April	September	8 ins.
„ *Tubergeniana*	Feb.–March	September	5 ins.
„ *verna*	April	October	4 ins.
Sternbergia Fischeriana	Feb.–March	September	9 ins.
„ *lutea*	Sept.–Oct.	March	8 ins.
Tulipa australis	April	October	6 ins.
„ *Batalini*	April	October	4 ins.
„ *biflora*	March–April	September	5 ins.
„ *chrysantha*	May	October	8 ins.
„ *dasystemon*	April–May	October	6 ins.
„ *Eichleri*	April	October	10 ins.
„ *Fosteriana*	April	October	8 ins.
„ *Greigii*	April	October	9 ins.
„ *Hageri*	April	October	9 ins.
„ *Kaufmanniana*	March–April	September	8 ins.
„ *Kolpakowskiana*	April	October	9 ins.
„ *linifolia*	May	October	6 ins.
„ *Maximowiczii*	April	October	6 ins.
„ *persica*	May	October	3 ins.
„ *primulina*	April	October	9 ins.
„ *pulchella*	March–April	September	4 ins.
„ *saxatilis*	May	October	9 ins.
„ *Tubergeniana*	May	October	10 ins.
„ *turkestanica*	March–April	September	6 ins.
„ *Wilsoniana*	May	October	3 ins.
Zephyranthes Andersonii	August	March	5 ins.
„ *atamasco*	May–June	September	7 ins.

Species	Flowering Time	Planting Time	Height
Zephyranthes candida	Aug.–Sept.	March	8 ins.
„ *carinata*	July-Aug.	March	6 ins.

HALF-HARDY BULBS

Anomatheca cruenta	July–Aug.	March	5 ins.
Babiana Bainesii	July	March	6 ins.
„ *disticha*	May–June	March	6 ins.
„ *plicata*	May–June	March	6 ins.
„ *rubro-cyanea*	May–June	March	3 ins.
Begonia multiflora	June–Nov.	May	6 ins.
Calochortus albus	June–July	March	8 ins.
„ *amoenus*	May–June	March	8 ins.
„ *Benthamii*	April–May	March	6 ins.
Haemanthus coccineus	Aug.–Sept.	April	9 ins.
Homeria collina	June–July	April	12 ins.
Rhodohypoxis baurii	May–June	March	3 ins.
Romulea sabulosa	May–June	March	3 ins.
Sparaxis tricolor	July–Aug.	April	10 ins.
Streptanthera cuprea	June–July	April	7 ins.
Tecophilaea cyanocrocus	March	September	3 ins.
Tritonia crocata	June–July	April	10 ins.

Index

Aconite, Winter (see *Eranthis*)
Allium, in the shrubbery, 27, 43;
  its culture, 127; its naturalising,
  27; species:
> *A. anceps*, 44, 127
> *A. cyaneum*, 72, 76, 127
> *A. flavum*, 43
> *A. karataviense*, 27, 30, 44, 57,
>   127
> *A. moly*, 27, 43, 44, 57, 127,
>   128, Pls. 4, 54
> *A. neapolitanum*, 27
> *A. ostrowskianum*, 57, 72, 128
> *A. pulchellum*, 43
> *A. ursinum*, 43, 44

Alpine garden, bulbs for, 68, their
  care, 73; cloches for the, 74;
  its construction, 65; its planting,
  68

Alpine house, bulbs for, 122
Anemone, for a chalky soil, 42; for
  bedding, 84; for naturalising, 29,
  128; its culture, 128; species and
  varieties:
> *A. apennina*, 42, 128
> *A. blanda*, 42, 122, 129
> *A. blanda rosea*, 42, 129
> *A. fulgens*, 129
> *A. nemorosa*, 29, 31, 49, 50
> *A. nemorosa Robinsoniana*, 49
> *A. nemorosa* 'Royal Blue', 29
> *A. palmata*, 130
> *A. ranunculoides*, 130
> *A. sylvestris*, 49, 50
> 'Poppy' anemones, 84, 128;
>   their planting, 85; varieties, 86

Anomatheca, in the alpine garden,
  73, 76, 96, 117; its culture, 118;
  species:
> *A. cruenta*, 73, 76, 96, 117
> *A. juncea*, 118
Anthericum, its culture, 130;
  species:
> *A. liliastrum*, 30, 130
Autumn Crocus (see *Colchicum*)

Babiana, its culture, 118; species:
> *B. Bainesii*, 118
> *B. disticha*, 118
> *B. plicata*, 118
> *B. rubro-cyanea*, 118
Begonia, *multiflora*, for a window
  box, 104; for bedding, 87; indoors, 118; its culture, 88, 118;
  varieties, 89
Bowles, E. A., 137, 138, 145, 146
Bowls, bulbs in, 111, 116
Brodiaea, for bedding, 82; in a
  trough garden, 93; indoors, 119;
  in the shrubbery, 47; its culture,
  131; species:
> *B. coccinea*, 47, 131, 132
> *B. crocea*, 47, 72, 76, 104, 132
> *B. grandiflora*, 30, 47, 72, 82,
>   132
> *B. ixioides*, 47, 132
> *B. laxa*, 82
> *B. minor*, 76, 93, 132
> *B. multiflora*, 47, 132
Bulbocodium, for a shrubbery, 45;
  its culture, 132; species:
> *B. vernum*, 45, 76, 133

185